ATTACK
AIRCRAFT

Roy Braybrook

Foulis

Haynes
®

A **FOULIS** Aviation Book

First published 1990

© Haynes Publishing Group 1990

Published by:
Haynes Publishing Group
Sparkford, Nr. Yeovil, Somerset
BA22 7JJ, England.

Haynes Publications Inc.
861 Lawrence Drive, Newbury Park,
California 91320, USA.

British Library Cataloguing in Publication data
Braybrook, Roy
  Attack aircraft of today.
  1. Fighter aeroplanes & attack aeroplanes
  I. Title
  623.74'64
  ISBN 0-85429-711-1

Library of Congress catalog card number
  89-85902

Editor: Mansur Darlington
Page Design: Mike King
Printed in England by: J.H. Haynes & Co. Ltd

Contents

Introduction

ATTACK AIRCRAFT OF TODAY is intended to serve as a companion volume to this author's previously published *Supersonic Fighter Development*. The latter emphasised the air-to-air role and thus excluded many interesting subsonic and transonic combat aircraft.

One of the perennial problems in discussions of aviation is that some key terms have no strict definitions. If definitions do exist, the terms are frequently misused, even by professionals in this field. For example, many people employ the term 'aircraft' purely in a fixed-wing sense. In this present work the author uses the term 'attack aircraft' to mean aeroplanes and helicopters that are employed in air-to-ground and anti-ship operations. Practically all bombers are excluded, the aim being to discuss comparatively small and manoeuvrable tactical aircraft.

Another recurring aviation problem is that operational flexibility provides a considerable overlap in aircraft roles. Thus, although there are clear distinctions between close air support and battlefield air interdiction, some aircraft are employed in both types of operation. Likewise, the attack mission is performed not only by dedicated attack aircraft such as the A-4, A-6, A7 and A-10, but also by derivatives of training aircraft, by supersonic strike fighters, and by what may be termed dual-role fighters, ie, aircraft that are equally good at the air-air and air-ground missions.

In order to lessen repetition and possible overlaps with the preceding *Supersonic Fighter Development* and *Military Training Aircraft Of Today*, this new work concentrates on dedicated tactical attack aircraft, and discusses in less detail the contributions made by fighters and trainer derivatives.

The first chapter provides a background on how the tactical attack mission has been carried out from the beginnings of military aviation. Subsequent chapters discuss today's attack aircraft according to the various categories to which they belong.

The dedicated fighter still represents the true cutting-edge of aerospace technology, but the successful development of a good attack aircraft nonetheless demands a great deal of careful planning and know-how. It is hoped that this work will add to the aircraft enthusiast's knowledge of the problems involved and the technologies employed in this increasingly important field.

Roy Braybrook

Chapter 1 **Operational Background**

LITTLE MORE THAN seven years after Orville Wright had made the world's first sustained flight in a heavier-than-air machine operating under its own power, the first real bomb was dropped from an aircraft in flight. Less than a year later, the first bomb was released in anger.

The attack technique was pioneered by Glen Curtiss in trials beginning on 30 June 1910, using dummy bombs against a target representing a battleship. However, the first release of an explosive device from an aircraft is believed to have occurred on 7 January 1911, from a two-seat Wright biplane flying near San Francisco. Shortly afterwards, the first bombsight was developed, and used successfully in a 1912 bombing contest.

War had not waited for such refinements. In the Italo-Turkish conflict in Tripolotania in North Africa, on 1 November 1911 an Italian Navy officer released four Cipelli grenades from an Etrich-built Taube monoplane flying over enemy positions. In the autumn of the following year the first Balkan War broke out, and Bulgarian aircraft dropped finned bombs on the town of Adrianople, then in Turkish hands.

Other attack developments prior to the outbreak of WWI included release trials with torpedoes. A 352 lb (160 kg) lightweight example was dropped from an Italian Navy Farman biplane in 1911, and a full-scale 14-inch (35.6 cm) 810 lb (367 kg) torpedo was released from an RNAS Short seaplane on 28 July 1914.

The declaration of war on 4 August 1914 brought a rapid expansion in the military use of aircraft, the initial emphasis on reconnaissance and artillery-spotting soon leading to the development of fighting scouts and bombers. The first bombing attack of the war was carried out on 14 August 1914 by two Voisin L pusher biplanes of the *Aéronautique Militaire*, each carrying 130 lb (59 kg) of small bombs on the floor of the observer's cockpit. The targets were the sheds near Metz that housed Zeppelins operating in support of the German Army. The airship was to prove a disaster in the army support role, but German Navy Zeppelins were a reconnaisance threat to the British Fleet and a bombing threat against Britain, the first such raid taking place on 19 January 1915.

The aerial torpedo was used operationally for the first time on 12 August 1915, when an RNAS Short 184 floatplane sank a 5000-ton Turkish cargo vessel in the Sea of Marmara. Other wartime attack developments included the first crude firebombs, and canisters containing up to 250 *fléchettes*, steel darts 5-6 inches

The Short 184 was the first aircraft to sink a ship by the use of a torpedo, the weapon employed being a 14-inch (35.6 cm) Whitehead. The aircraft pictured (N.1091) was from a batch of 10 with 240 hp Renault engines. (Shorts)

(13-15 cm) long, which proved very effective against cavalry and troops in the open.

One of the more interesting attack developments of WWI was trench-strafing, which was regarded (like the first British Army tanks) as a possible means to break the deadlock on the ground. It was, however, soon found that the advantage generally rested with the men on the ground. The fast-firing machine gun that had produced the stalemate for the infantry was also quite effective against a low-flying aircraft moving at only 100 mph (160 km/hr). On the British side, Sopwith Camels and D.H.5s were employed in trench-strafing, but losses ran at horrific levels (around 30 per cent each day).

In November 1917 the RFC issued a requirement for a dedicated ground attack aircraft, to be fitted with armour plate in critical areas. It was to have one machine gun firing directly ahead, and one or two more firing forwards and 35-55 degrees below the horizontal. One Camel was modified to this TF.1 standard, with armour and two Lewis guns firing at 45 degrees downwards through the cockpit floor. Another was tested with an inverted periscopic sight, but the use of downward-firing guns proved impractical for single-seaters. Trench-strafing modifications for operational Camels were restricted to 12 mm of armour plate below the pilot's seat.

In January 1918 the War Office invited Sopwith to make new proposals for a ground attack aircraft with three guns (later reduced to two) and four 20 lb (9.1 kg) bombs. The resulting **TF.2 Salamander** was a Snipe-derivative with 605 lb (275 kg) of armour, which increased its empty weight by 50 per cent. This severely reduced its manoeuvrability and the enthusiasm with which squadron pilots received it. The first two units were still forming when the Armistice was signed in November 1918, and the Salamander was retired in 1922.

On the German side the obvious candidates for close support duties had been Junkers all-metal aircraft, which avoided the problem of fabric coverings

tearing when damaged. The company had produced the first practical all-metal aircraft in 1915: the 'Tin Donkey', skinned with smooth tin plate. Two years later Junkers was using in corrugated form the Durener Metallwerke's aluminium alloy (Duralumin), which had been discovered accidentally by Alfred Wilm in 1909 while trying to produce an aluminium alloy suitable for cartridge cases.

The first Dural aircraft was the **Junkers J.I.** biplane of 1917, which had 5 mm of armour around the engine and both crew members. This plating weighed

Photographed in May 1918, this Sopwith Salamander was a derivative of the Snipe with a 200 hp Bentley rotary engine, intended for trench-strafing. (BAe)

The Junkers J.I of 1917 had armour protection for the engine and cockpit. (MBB)

1036 lb (470 kg), a penalty reflected in the empty weight of 3724 lb (1690 kg) and the maximum weight of 4800 lb (2175 kg). The J.I. was normally armed with two forward-firing Spandaus and a flexibly mounted Parabellum on the rim of the rear cockpit, although some early examples had two downward-firing Parabellums operated by the observer. As in the case of the Camel, this arrangement was found to be unworkable. The first of 200 J.Is entered service in 1918.

The J.I may well have been the best German armoured aircraft of WWI, but the best German ground attack aircraft was considered to be the **Junkers CL.I** monoplane. Likewise built in corrugated Dural, it first flew in May 1918, but took little part in the war. Being unarmoured, its maximum weight was only 2326 lb (1055 kg). Like the J.I, it had two Spandaus and one Parabellum, but it also had external fuselage racks for stick grenades, which were dropped by the observer. Some of the 47 CL.Is built subsequently served in Estonia, Finland and Lithuania.

The Junkers CL.I was regarded by some experts as the best German ground attack aircraft to see operational service in WWI. (MBB)

Between The Wars
During the 1920s there was a general hiatus in military aviation development. For example, Britain's RAF was mainly concerned with policing overseas territories such as Iraq and the North-West Frontier of India. This role was largely

performed by WWI-generation two-seat general purpose aircraft such as the D.H.9A and Bristol Fighter F.2B, which remained in service until 1931 and 1932 respectively. They were replaced by more multi-role biplanes, such as the Westland Wapiti. The Hawker Hart fast light bomber biplane entered service in 1920, to be superseded by the Fairey Battle monoplane in 1937 and the twin-engined Bristol Blenheim in 1938.

The performance of naval aircraft was initially limited by the 27,000 ton displacement restriction on carriers agreed under the 1922 Washington Naval Treaty, but in 1935 this limit was removed, due to the growing threat of war. The first torpedo-bomber to be designed from the outset for carrier operation was the **Sopwith Cuckoo,** which was built in small numbers just before the end of WWI. It carried an 18-inch (46 cm) diameter Mk IX 1000 lb (454 kg) torpedo. Six Cuckoos were presented to the Imperial Japanese Navy in 1922.

The Cuckoo was followed by the Blackburn Dart, Ripon and Baffin. In 1936 these torpedo-bombers began to be replaced by the **Fairey Swordfish,** which could carry a 1610 lb (730 kg) 18-inch (46 cm) torpedo. The first British monoplane attack aircraft was the **Blackburn Skua** of 1938, which combined the roles of dive-bomber and fighter.

High-angle dive-bombing was probably the most important attack develop-

When the Hawker Hart entered service with No 33 Sqn of the RAF in 1930, it outperformed most contemporary single-seat fighters. This example in the RAF Museum was flown postwar with the registration G-ABMR. (Roy Braybrook)

ment of the 1930s. It was pioneered by the US Navy, while the US Army concentrated on strategic bombing. The latter is outside the scope of this book, but one of the Army's early developments is relevant, in the sense that the Martin MB-2 biplane was used in some important bombing trials against naval vessels. The MB-2 is today best remembered as the platform from which Brig-Gen 'Billy' Mitchell bombed and sank the ex-German 22,800-ton battleship *Ostfriesland* on 21 July 1921.

This test (and a 1923 series in which three old US battleships were sunk) demonstrated that even a heavily-armoured warship could be destroyed, if it could be hit by suitable bombs. Doubts remained whether the same effects could be produced by aerial torpedoes, which were much less effective than those used by destroyers and submarines. Some experts felt that Britain's battleships could not be sunk by 18-inch (46 cm) torpedoes, and were thus safe against this form of aerial attack. In the event, in December 1941 the battleship *Prince of Wales* and the battle-cruiser *Repulse* were sunk by the land-based, twin-engined Japanese Navy Mitsubishi G3M2 ('Nell') and G4M1 ('Betty') using heavy torpedoes and operating over a radius of 350 nm (650 km).

While doubts hung over the effectiveness of aerial torpedoes in the 1920s and 1930s, there was no question about the lethality of armour-piercing bombs, provided they could be delivered accurately enough to hit the target. To translate Mitchell's level bombing on a static target into an operational reality (ie, with a fast, turning ship) a very precise delivery was essential.

In level releases, bombs are scattered in an elliptical pattern around the aiming point, the longest dimension of the ellipse being along the flight path of the aircraft. If bombs are released in a dive, the along-track errors are reduced. In the extreme case of a vertical dive, the bombs are distributed in a small circle. The lower the release, the smaller that circle.

What the US Navy required for effective anti-ship attacks was therefore an aircraft that could make very steep dives without building up excessive speed, and was stressed for a low level high-G recovery. The development of such aircraft in America was to have profound effects abroad, most notably on the Japanese Navy and the German Air Force. Aside from being essential for effective ballistic attacks on ships, dive bombing was also of special value in close support operations by the USMC and in precise tactical attacks by the USAAC.

The development of dive-bombers is well illustrated by the **Curtiss Helldiver** series, which began with the USMC's two-seat OC-1 or F8C-1 biplane of 1928. The Helldiver name was also applied to the SBC biplane of 1937 and the SB2C monoplane, which entered service in 1942. The other important USN dive-bomber of the period was the **Douglas SBD Dauntless** of 1941, originally designed by Northrop (at the time a Douglas subsidiary) as the BT-2, and using that company's split-flap airbrake. The initial production Dauntless was the SBD-1 of late 1941, with a 1000 hp R-1820-52 radial engine, a maximum speed of 246 mph (394 km/hr) and a maximum take-off weight of 8157 lb (3700 kg). Other US dive-bombers included the **Northrop A-17** of 1935 and the **Vultee Vengenance** of 1942, both produced for the US Army and for export.

During the 1920s Germany had no air force, but a small training and trials unit was maintained at Lipezk in the Soviet Union, where tests are said to have

The Douglas SBD Dauntless dive bomber of 1941. Note the perforated airbrakes. (Harry Gann, McDonnell Douglas) 1/6.

The Northrop XBT-2 acted as the prototype for the Douglas Dauntless. (Northrop Corp)

The Northrop A-17 entered service with the US Army in 1935. The later A-17A had a retractable main gear. (Northrop Corp)

included dive-bombing. Japan also became interested in the concept, and in 1931 funded Heinkel to develop a two-seat dive-bomber, the **He 50**.

During a visit to the US in 1933, Ernst Udet, a famous German fighter ace and stunt pilot, who in 1936 became head of the *Luftwaffe* technical office, saw a demonstration by a Curtiss dive-bomber, presumably the original biplane Helldiver. Udet was so impressed that he became a strong advocate of dive-bombing, and arranged for Germany to buy two Helldivers, which were delivered in late 1933.

The Henschel Hs 123 was the German Luftwaffe's last combat biplane and its first dedicated Stuka. (Henschel Flugzeug-Werke GmbH Kassel)

Employment of the Hs 123 in Spain was preceded by use of the He 51 in the close support role. (MBB)

The existence of the new *Luftwaffe* was formally announced only on 5 May 1935. The Air Staff had already had its first sight of dive-bombing in a demonstration by Udet, using a modified Focke-Wulf Fw 56. The service had also purchased a small number of He 50s for trials, and had initiated a two-phase dive-bomber (Stuka = *Sturzkampfflugzeug*) programme. The first production type was to be the radial-engined **Henschel Hs 123,** the service's last combat biplane. It made its public début on 8 May 1935, with Gen Udet at the controls, and production deliveries began in the late summer of 1936. The Hs 123 was followed in the spring of 1937 by deliveries of the infamous Junkers Ju 87, which had first flown in 1935.

The first dedicated Stuka unit was an offshoot of a covert army co-operation unit, the so-called *Reklamestaffel Mitteldeutschland* (Advertising Squadron, Central Germany) at Berlin-Staaken. On 1 October 1935 a new trials and training flight was formed, initially equipped with He 50s and Arado Ar 65s, and bearing the harmless title *Fliegergruppe Schwerin*. The unit subsequently became the first of six *Stukagruppen*, designated I/StG 162 and equipped with the Hs 123.

Following the outbreak of the Spanish Civil War, which ran from 13 July 1936 to 28 March 1939, five Hs 123s were in December 1936 seconded to the Legion Condor, which was assisting the Nationalist forces of General Franco. This secondment followed the successful use of the He 51 biplane fighter, experimentally fitted with bombs. The Hs 123s formed a special flight of *Kampfgruppe 88* (a Ju 52/3m unit), and were used in conventional close support operations, rather than dive-bombing.

In December 1937 three of the new Ju 87A-1s from StG 163 arrived in Spain, forming the *'Jolanthe Kette'*, which had its operational début on 17 January 1938. The Ju 87 was used for dive-bombing, though the A-1s suffered technical problems, and in October 1938 were replaced by five Ju 87B-1s, which built up a good reputation for precise weapons delivery.

Another dive-bomber used in Spain was Italy's Breda 65, which joined the

In Spain the He 111 was used in tactical bombing operations. This later Merlin-engined CASA C-2111E was employed as a troop transport under the designation T8B. Serialed T8B-124, it was photographed at Blackbushe in 1976 with the UK registration G-BDYA, following purchase by Douglas Arnold. (Roy Braybrook)

The Junkers Ju 52/3m was first employed operationally as a tactical bomber in Spain. This later CASA-built C-352 (serial T2B-212) was photographed at Blackbushe in 1976. (Roy Braybrook)

Aviazione Legionaria in April 1937. Beginning in the previous month, the He 51 was relegated to ground attack, since its performance fell below the standard needed in air combat.

One significant event in that war was the destruction of the old Basque city of Guernica on 26 April 1937 by around 40 He 111Bs, Ju 52/3ms and Savoia-Marchetti SM 79s, ostensibly to take out a key bridge over the River Oca, some 10 miles (16 km) behind the lines. Incendiary bombs were used, and about 1000 civilians were killed, while the bridge survived unscathed.

Some lessons learned in Spain proved misleading, as fortunately proved true in regard to predicting casualties in the bombing of major cities. The dive-bomber's success in Spain was to be repeated by the *Luftwaffe* on a large scale in the early months of WWII, but then attrition shot up to unacceptable levels as the Ju 87 came up against fighters of vastly superior performance.

World War Two

The **Ju 87** was the classic high-angle dive-bomber. It typically attacked from an approach at around 115 mph (185 km/hr) at 5000 ft (1500 m), diving at 60-80 degrees with wing-mounted airbrakes extended and its large propeller in fine pitch, releasing bombs at around 210 mph (335 km/hr). In pulling out the Ju 87 would reach perhaps 245 mph (392 km/hr), but go no lower than 2000 ft (600 m) to avoid debris thrown up by its bombs. Later aircraft would make wind allowances according to the impact points of the ordnance dropped by the lead pilot.

The standard Stuka at the outbreak of WWII was the Ju 87B-1, with a 1100 hp liquid-cooled Junkers Jumo engine. It typically carried a single 550 or 1100 lb (250 or 500 kg) bomb on a ventral 'trapeze' that swung it clear of the propeller. Sirens were carried on the undercarriage legs to frighten those on the ground. Three 7.9 mm machine guns were fitted: two MG17s in the wings and a flexibly-mounted MG15 fired by the observer. The Ju 87B-1 had a maximum weight of 9370 lb (4250 kg) and a maximum level speed of 232 mph (370 km/hr) at 13,500 ft (4100 m).

Both the Ju 87 and Hs 123 were used with outstanding success in the invasion of Poland in August 1939, and in the April-May 1940 onslaughts against Norway, Belgium, Holland and France. These operations were conducted mainly in good weather, hence cloud ceilings posed few problems. After the end of the French campaign the old Hs 123 was phased out of service in the West, but from the time

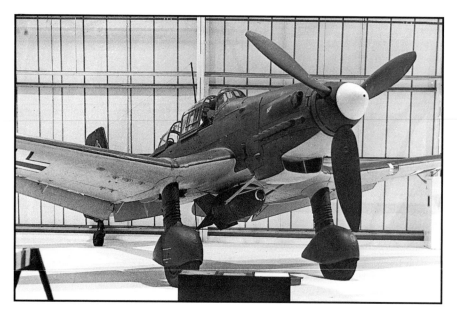

Although exhibited in the Battle of Britain Museum in dive bomber configuration, it is believed that this aircraft (WkNr 494083), having originally been built as a Ju 87B-5 Trop for night operations in North Africa, was later converted to Ju 87G-2 tank-buster standard, with two 37 mm BK 3,7 cannon under the wings, and the airbrakes deleted. (Roy Braybrook)

Seen here in side view, the Ju 87B was the standard type in service with Stuka units at the outbreak of WWII. (MBB)

of Dunkirk the Ju 87 was operating within reach of RAF fighters based in SE England, and the vulnerability of the slow-flying Stuka was immediately apparent.

Stuka losses continued during the attacks on Channel convoys and in the Battle of Britain. In September 1940 some Messerschmitt Me 109Es began to be used in the fighter-bomber (*Jabo = Jagdbomber*) role in hit-and-run attacks against towns in southern England. They experienced much lower losses, but, operating in small numbers, produced only minor damage.

Stuka successes nevertheless continued in attacks on Allied convoys in the Mediterranean and against Malta, and in the invasions of Yugoslavia and Greece. Conversely, when Germany attempted to push British forces out of North Africa, Stukas came up against RAF fighters and again sustained heavy losses. By late 1942 the Ju 87s were being replaced by Focke Wulf Fw 190 *Jabos*, and a year later, when German forces were retreating up Italy, these Fw 190s were escorted by fighters.

The Stuka's greatest success of WWII was probably attained in the initial attack on the Soviet Union in June 1941, when it was estimated that 1800 Russian aircraft were destroyed on the first day alone, mostly on the ground. On the other hand, as German forces advanced deeper, what was needed was an effective way to kill individual tanks. A bomb required a direct hit, which was seldom possible.

The alternative solution was to attack with heavy cannon firing armour-piercing ammunition, an approach adopted for both the Ju 87 and for conventional ground attack aircraft. The Ju 87G-1 was given a pair of 37 mm BK 3,7 cannon, and a similar armament was applied to the Me 110 and Ju 88P in ground attack units (*Schlachtgeschwader*, abbreviated to SchG or simply SG). The SGs had been introduced in mid-1941, initially with the Hs 123 and Me 109E, but they later had a variety of combat aircraft, notably the Hs 129.

As with many 'Emils', the Battle of Britain Museum example (WkNr 4101) was converted in the field to Me 109E-3b fighter-bomber standard. Prior to being forced down at RAF Manston, it was operated first by 6/JG52 and then by 2/JG51, based at Wissant in Belgium. It is shown in the markings of 1/JG51. (Roy Braybrook)

The role of the Stuka was largely taken over by the Focke-Wulf Fw 190, which was also built in an underground factory at Cravant in France under the designation NC.900. This example shown at the *Musée de l'Air* is No 62 from a total of 64 constructed at this SNCAC plant. (Roy Braybrook)

The Henschel Hs 129 was a heavily armed and armoured tank-buster developed for the Eastern Front. (Henschel Flugzeug-Werke GmbH Kassel)

The Blackburn Skua was the Fleet Air Arm's first monoplane. This second prototype (K5179), like the first (K5178), flew with the Mercury IX engine, but production Skuas had the 905 hp Bristol Perseus XII sleeve-valve engine. (BAe)

The **Hs 129**, of which Henschel says 1160 were built, had an armoured front fuselage, two 700 hp Gnome-Rhone radial engines, a gross weight of 11,250 lb (5100 kg), and a maximum speed of 256 mph (410 km/hr). The Hs 129B-1 series combined automatic weapons with a small bomb load, but the B-2 relied on guns. Its armour-piercing cannon grew in calibre from 30 to 37 mm. and ultimately 75 mm, a single BK 7,5 guns being fitted in a jettisonable fairing under the Hs 129B-2/R4. The Hs 129 proved quite effective against Soviet tanks, but from late 1942 it was augmented in the SGs by bomb-carrying Fw 190s, which later used cluster weapons and rocket projectiles.

Following the Normandy landings, Allied air superiority in the West was such that even the Fw 190 could not be operated in ground attack without heavy losses. This led to the formation of night attack units (*Nachtschlachtgruppen* or NSGs), which operated under radio control, and only at night or in bad visibility. The NSGs played a major part in Operation Bodenplatte of 1 January 1945, when massed low level attacks were made on Allied airfields in the Low Countries.

The *Luftwaffe's* situation on the Eastern Front was less desperate, but Ju 87 units converted to the Fw 190 as quickly as the demands of the fighter wings allowed. The Ju 87s, over 5500 of which had been built, were then passed to the NSGs, joining a mixture of obsolete types. Other types of attack unit were combined together in October 1943, when the StGs, SGs, and SKGs (*Schnellkampfgeschwader* or fast attack wings) were reorganised as SGs. Attacks were made in relatively shallow dives, and development emphasised better weapons, rather than specialised aircraft. These weapons later included cluster bombs with anti-personnel and hollow-charge bomblets, and the *Panzerschreck* and *Panzerblitz* rocket projectiles. In trials predating the current German VBW weapon system, three Hs 129s were fitted with six-barrel 77 mm devices that fired projectiles downward when flying over a tank triggered a photo-electric cell.

Although Goering's *Luftwaffe* soon abandoned the use of steep dive attacks, it remained a useful tactic against ships. This was particularly true for aircraft operating in the clear skies of the Pacific, whereas in other areas a high-angle dive was often ruled out by a low cloud-base.

While the US Navy, with its larger number of aircraft, could afford to use specialised dive-bombers, Britain's Fleet Air Arm (FAA) had traditionally favoured dual- or multi-role aircraft. For example, the **Blackburn Skua** performed both as a dive-bomber and fighter. Skuas from the Home Fleet shot down the first enemy aircraft (a Dornier Do 18 off Norway on 26 September 1939), and shortly afterwards Skuas from the Orkneys dive-bombed and sank the cruiser *Koenigsberg* near Bergen.

The best-remembered action by FAA aircraft was, however, the night attack by ageing **Fairey Swordfish** torpedo-spotter-reconnaissance biplanes against the Italian fleet in Taranto harbour on 11 November 1940. Flying from HMS *Illustrious*, 11 Swordfish with torpedoes, supported by nine more carrying bombs and flares, put out of action three battleships (two of which sank), a cruiser, two destroyers, and two auxiliary ships.

Aircraft of the FAA were also effective in interdicting Axis supplies to North Africa: Malta-based Swordfish and Albacores sank 400,000 tons of shipping, largely in radar-assisted night torpedo attacks. They also disabled several major

The Fairey Swordfish of the RN
Historic Aircraft Flight (serial
LS326, registration G-AJVH), was
photographed at RNAS Yeovilton
in 1974. (Roy Braybrook)

Over 190 Skuas were ordered in
July 1936. This example (L2883) is
shown with dive-brakes
lowered. (BAe)

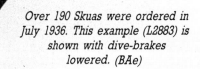

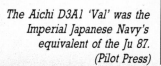

The Aichi D3A1 'Val' was the
Imperial Japanese Navy's
equivalent of the Ju 87.
(Pilot Press)

enemy warships that were later finished off by naval gunfire: in 1941 Italy lost three cruisers and Germany lost the battleship *Bismarck* in this way.

On the Japanese side, the greatest achievement by naval air power was the surprise attack on Pearl Harbour and nearby facilities on 7 December 1941, an action possibly inspired by Taranto. In a dawn strike from Admiral Nagumo's six carriers, positioned 240 nm (440 km) north of the Hawaian Islands, a total of 353 aircraft were launched in two waves. In attacks beginning at 0755 hr local time, they destroyed or damaged 18 US warships or auxiliaries and 349 aircraft, and killed or wounded 3581 military personnel, though they lost 29 aircraft (ie, 8.2 per cent). The aircraft used were the **Aichi D3A1 'Val'** dive-bomber, the Nakajima B5N2 'Kate' torpedo-bomber, and the Mitsubishi A6M2 Model 21 'Zeke' fighter.

The 'Val' might be regarded as Japan's naval equivalent of the Ju 87, though only the airbrakes were copied directly from that aircraft. It had a 1000 hp radial engine, a loaded weight of 8047 lb (3650 kg), and a maximum speed of 240 mph (385 km/hr). Defence was provided by three 7.7 mm machine guns: two in the

The Nakajima B5N2 'Kate' was the principal torpedo-bomber employed in the strike on Pearl Harbour. (Pilot Press)

cowling and one mounted flexibly at the rear of the cabin. Bombload was normally one 550 lb (250 kg) under the fuselage and two 132 lb (60 kg) under the wings.

The Japanese enjoyed a straight run of successes in the first months of the war in the Pacific, but then the tide turned. On 18 April 1942 16 **North American B-25B** Mitchells of the US Army, operating in a one-way mission from the US Navy carrier *Hornet*, attacked the Japanese cities of Tokyo, Osaka, Kobe and Nagoya.

In the following month the first naval battle took place in which no shots were fired between ships, all the losses being inflicted by carrier-borne aircraft. In this Battle of the Coral Sea each side lost one carrier and had another severely damaged, but the US could afford this better than Japan. One month later in the Battle of Midway Island, four Japanese carriers were destroyed by dive-bombers from USN carriers, while only one American carrier was lost.

In June 1944 a further Japanese carrier was lost to USN aircraft in the Battle of the Philippine Sea, and in October that year four more Japanese carriers were sunk in the Battle of Leyte Gulf. Japanese naval aviation, which was of crucial importance in maintaining a grip on the Pacific islands, had been virtually wiped out, and largely by carrier-based USN aircraft, using dive-bombing and torpedo attacks.

The TBF-1 was the first production model of the Grumman Avenger, deliveries of which began at the end of January 1942. (Grumman Corp)

Avengers were also built by
General Motors under the
designation TBM, pictured here
in 1945. (US Navy photo, via
Grumman Corp)

Aside from the aircraft mentioned earlier, one of the most important contributions in this campaign was that of the **Grumman Avenger** torpedo-bomber, a three-seat aircraft with a 1700 hp Wright R-2600 radial engine. The Avenger grew to a weight of 18,250 lb (8275 kg), and had a maximum speed of 276 mph (440 km/hr). It had an internal weapon bay to accommodate a torpedo or a 2000 lb (910 kg) bomb, and three machine guns for defence, including one 12.7 mm in a powered dorsal turret. The prototype flew on 1 August 1941, and the Avenger entered service at the Battle of Midway.

Rocket Projectiles

As demonstrated by German anti-tank operations on the Eastern Front, and by their British equivalents in North Africa and Burma (with **Hurricane IIDs** armed with two 40 mm Vickers S guns under the wings) heavy cannon represented an effective means to disable armoured vehicles. An even more potent weapon was found to be the rocket projectile (RP), which offered longer firing range and greater destructive power. This concept represented in the early 1940s just as major an advance as the high-angle dive had offered in the 1930s.

The Hawker Hurricane IID, armed with a pair of 40 mm Vickers 'S' cannon, was used to good effect both in North Africa and Burma. (BAe, via Michael Stroud)

It is generally accepted that the first of the Allies to employ RPs in the ground attack role was the Soviet Union, using 82 and 132 mm missiles on the **Ilyushin Il-2.** Whether this is correct, the Il-2 was certainly one of the best attack aircraft of WWII: the Russians go further, and claim that no other aircraft played such a decisive role in the conflict. Some 35,000 were built, and Stalin said in late 1941 (in

The Ilyushin Il-2 is shown here in its later two-seat form, the second crew member having been found invaluable both as a gunner and observer. (Pilot Press)

trying to boost production) that it was 'as essential to the Red Army as air and bread'.

The Il-2 began as a two-seater, the BSh-2 (*Bronirovannii Shturmovik*, or armoured attack aircraft), and in this form flew in late 1939. Nonetheless, it entered service in the summer of 1941 as a single-seater, the gunner being removed to increase fuel space. It had a gross weight of 11,683 lb (5300 kg) and a liquid-cooled 1665 hp engine giving a clean maximum speed of 292 mph (467 km/hr). Some 1540 lb (700 kg) of armour protected the engine, radiator, oil cooler, fuel tanks and the pilot. The Il-2 was armed with two 20 mm cannon and two 7.62 mm machine guns and carried a bomb load of 1100-1325 lb (500-600 kg). It could carry eight RS-82 or RS-132 rockets in combination with four 220 lb (100 kg) bombs.

To reduce the Il-2's vulnerability to opposing fighters, a two-seat version (Il-2M) was then produced, the gunner having a single 12.7 mm machine gun. In this form it entered service in late 1942, and soon demonstrated that it required no fighter escort. Other improvements included the replacement of the 20 mm cannon by two 37 mm, a 1750 hp engine, and a weapon load of 200 5.5 lb (2.5 kg) bomblets in four Der-50 containers. Armour rose to a total of 2183 lb (990 kg).

Britain initially developed the 3-inch (76 mm) rocket for ground-based air defence use, but (possibly inspired by the Soviet example) this weapon was also applied in modified form to aircraft such as Hawker's Hurricane and Typhoon. These RPs were originally carried on launching rails (which proved unnecessary), and could be fitted with either a 25 lb (11.3 kg) solid warhead or a 60 lb (27.2 kg) explosive type. The old 'drainpipe' was inaccurate, but during WWII it was fired at very short ranges (down to 300 metres), which enabled it to be used effectively not only against armoured vehicles but also against ships and trains.

The Hurricane and Typhoon were both designed as fighters, then quickly relegated to ground attack due to performance deficiencies. Both wings had been designed in the light of advice from the National Physical Laboratory at Teddington, that no improvement in drag would be obtained by reducing the thickness/chord ratio below 20 per cent. It was later discovered that this quite erroneous advice arose from measurements made in a wind tunnel that suffered from a high degree of turbulence. In the meantime, the Hurricane and Typhoon had entered service in 1937 and late 1941 respectively, with wings that were far thicker than the optimum for the fighter role.

The Hurricane performed usefully in a number of roles, but the Typhoon was a far better ground attack aircraft, carrying a heavier punch and operating at a far more survivable speed. To illustrate this point, the **Hurricane IID** with 1280 hp Rolls-Royce Merlin XX and a gross weight of only 7850 lb (3560 kg) carried two 40 mm cannon, but had a maximum speed of only 286 mph (458 km/hr). In contrast, the **Typhoon,** with a 2200 hp Napier Sabre and a gross weight of 13,250 lb (6000 kg) could deliver eight RPs or two 1000 lb (454 kg) bombs, and had a clean maximum of 412 mph (659 km/hr).

The Typhoon came into its own around the time of the Normandy landings, in interdicting supplies to German coastal defences and later in attacking tanks opposing Allied ground forces. At one stage RAF Typhoons were destroying 150 locomotives per month, using rockets and bombs. During the fighting to break out from the beach-head, Typhoons destroyed 137 German tanks in a single operation.

American land-based fighters such as the North American P-51 Mustang, the Republic P-47 Thunderbolt, and the Lockheed P-38 Lighning were all used in ground attack missions. Some employed 4.5 inch (114 mm) M8 RPs in an M10 launcher, consisting of three tubes fastened together. Navy fighters such as the Grumman F6F Hellcat later used the 5-inch (127 mm) HVAR (high velocity aircraft rocket).

The greatest US fighter-bomber of WWII was arguably the **Vought F4U Corsair,** which went on to fly close support missions for the USMC in Korea in the early 1950s. Broadly comparable to Britain's Hawker Sea Fury, which first flew on 1 September 1944 in land-based form and entered service in 1947, the Corsair first flew in May 1940, with deliveries following early in 1943. It was initially judged unsuited to carrier operation, and naval clearance was granted only in late 1944.

Like the Ju 87, the Corsair had a cranked wing, primarily to keep its 13 ft 4 in (4.06 m) propeller clear of the deck. The ultimate WWII version of Vought's 'bent-wing bird' was the F4U-4, which had a 2100 hp P&W R-2800 radial engine, a gross weight of 14,670 (6653 kg) and a maximum speed of 446 mph (714 km/hr). The F4U-4 retained the six 12.7 mm machine guns of the original, but it could also carry eight HVARs in combination with two 1000 lb (454 kg) bombs, or two massive 11.75 inch (300 mm) 'Tiny Tim' rockets.

Before leaving this discussion of attack aircraft of WWII, there are various points worth making. Firstly, what was needed was evidently a combination of performance, warload and damage-tolerance, rather than placing all the emphasis on just one of these parameters. Secondly, if a single-engined aircraft was to perform well in this role, then it needed a great deal of power, ie 2000 hp

The RAF's use of RPs is illustrated by this Hawker Hurricane Mk IV (serial BP173), a ground attack variant with a 1620 hp R-R Merlin 24 or 27. (BAe, via Michael Stroud)

The Hawker Typhoon, exemplified here by a Mk IB (EK497), was probably the best British ground attack aircraft of WWII. (BAe, via Michael Stroud).

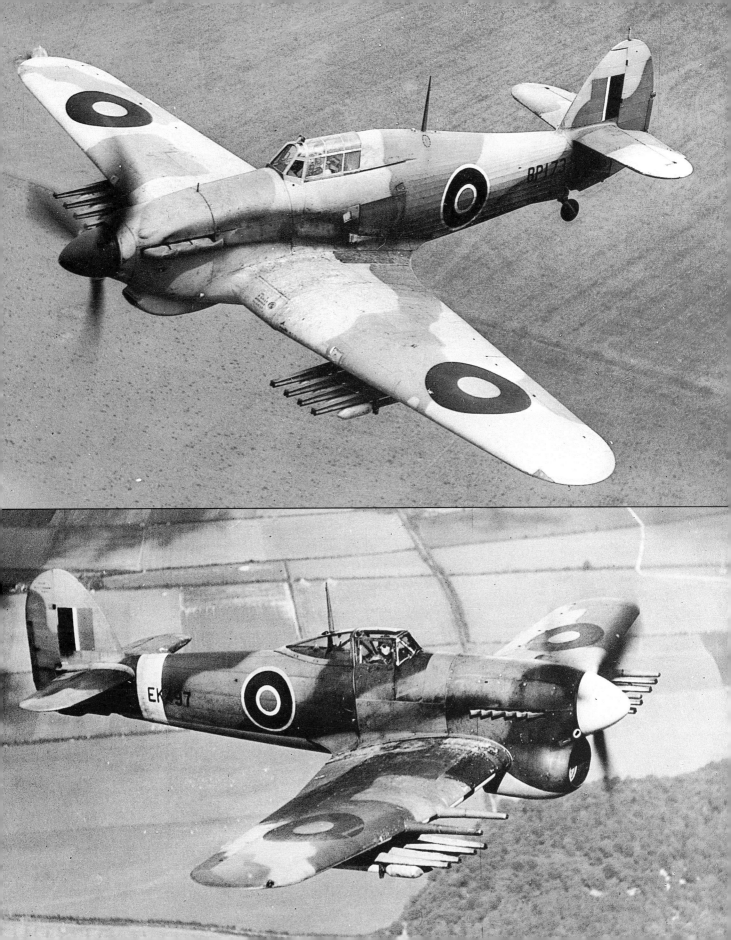

rather than the 1000 hp that was available at the start of the conflict. Thirdly, a good warload-radius performance demanded a comparatively large aircraft, such as the Corsair rather than the Me 109.

If the Corsair really was the best single-engined fighter-bomber of WWII, some credit was due to the US Navy's prewar emphasis on air-cooled radial engines for dependability in long sorties over water. Such engines were far more tolerant of combat damage than the liquid-cooled powerplants favoured by the US Army for minimum drag. On the other hand, (with the exception of the Army's Bell P-39 Airacobra, designed to carry a 37 mm cannon) all the US services were slow in switching from 12.7 mm machine guns to cannon. The US Navy introduced 20 mm guns with the Douglas AD-1 Skyraider and Grumman F9F Panther only in the late 1940s, and the USAF followed with the 20 mm M39 revolver cannon on the North American F-100 Super Sabre in 1954.

The Vought F4U-1D Corsair had provisions for two 1000 lb (454 kg) bombs or eight HVARs under the wings. This is one of several preserved, serial 92468, registration NX9964Z. (LTV Aircraft Products Group)

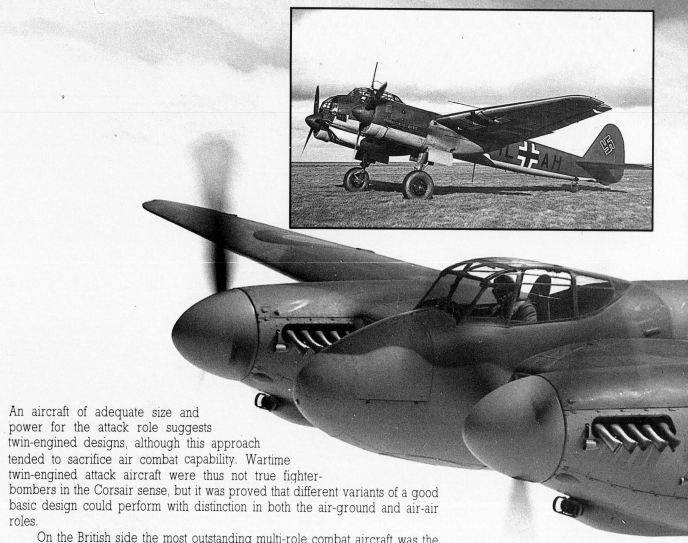

An aircraft of adequate size and
power for the attack role suggests
twin-engined designs, although this approach
tended to sacrifice air combat capability. Wartime
twin-engined attack aircraft were thus not true fighter-
bombers in the Corsair sense, but it was proved that different variants of a good
basic design could perform with distinction in both the air-ground and air-air
roles.

On the British side the most outstanding multi-role combat aircraft was the
two-seat **de Havilland Mosquito,** which first flew in November 1940, and
excelled both as a light bomber and as a night fighter. The first bomber version
was the Mk IV, which had a maximum weight of 20,870 lb (9465 kg) and two
Rolls-Royce Merlin XXIs, giving a maximum speed of 380 mph (608 km/hr).
Normal warload was four 500 lb (227 kg) bombs, though some Mk IVs were
modified to take the 4000 lb (1815 kg) 'blockbuster'.

The other great multi-role aircraft of the war was the **Junkers Ju 88,** which
first flew in December 1936. It had a crew of four, and entered service in the
summer of 1939. The first major series was the Ju 88A-1, with two 1200 hp Jumo
211B engines giving a maximum speed of 286 mph (485 km/hr). Its normal bomb
load of 3970 lb (1800 kg) produced a gross weight of 27,500 lb (12,470 kg), making
it substantially heavier than a Mosquito. Later ground attack variants included the
Ju 88P-1 with one 75 mm cannon, and the Ju 88P-2 with two of 37 mm. Equipped

*The de Havilland Mosquito was
arguably the best British
multi-role combat aircraft of
WWII. This T3 variant (RR299,
registration G-ASKH) is preserved
by British Aerospace at Hatfield.
(BAe)*

with two 1750 hp Jumo 213E-1s, the Ju
88S-3 *Schnellbomber* reached a maximum speed of
371 mph (594 km/hr). Like the Bristol Beaufighter and its postwar
successor the Brigand, the Ju 88 was also used in torpedo attacks on shipping.

There was no real US equivalent of the Mosquito, although the P-38 Lightning
was used in many roles, including torpedo attacks and night fighting. Where
America excelled was in the development of light/medium bombers, such as the
North American B-25, which first flew in August 1940, with deliveries beginning
in the following year. The first large-scale production model was the B-25C, with
1350 hp R-2600 radials and a maximum speed of 284 mph (455 km/hr). A
bombload of 3000 lb (1360 kg) could be carried internally, giving a gross weight
of 34,000 lb (15,420 kg). Later versions included the B-25H anti-shipping model
with one 75 mm gun and no less than 14 machine guns.

In the light bomber category, Germany's ultimate fast bomber was the **Arado
Ar 234** *Blitz* (Lightning), which flew in June 1943. The production Ar 234B entered
service in the autumn of 1944 with two 1980 lb (900 kg) Junkers Jumo 004B

Insets: *The German equivalent of
the Mosquito was the Junkers
Ju 88. The Ju 88A shown here
entered service in 1939 and was
employed in attacks on the UK in
September of that year. (MBB)*

turbojets and a maximum speed of 460 mph (738 km/hr). It had a bomb-load of 3300 lb (1500 kg) and a gross weight of 20,613 lb (9350 kg), comparable to that of the Mosquito.

One of a group of North American B-25 Mitchells that appeared at Blackbushe in 1978 in connection with the filming of Hanover Street. *(Roy Braybrook)*

Early Postwar Developments

Although Germany had led the way, the postwar transition to jet-powered attack aircraft was a slow one. Some good piston-engined designs had flown (or even entered service) just before the end of the war, and there was no immediate motivation to discard them and spend funds on their jet-powered equivalents.

For example, the **Douglas A-26 Invader** had flown in 1942 and entered service with the USAAF in Europe in November 1944. Redesignated the B-26 in 1948, the Invader served with the USAF throughout the Korean War (1950-53), and was later used in COIN (counter-insurgency) operations in the Congo and SE Asia. The ultimate Invader was the B26K conversion by On Mark Engineering, with 2500 hp R-2800s, a maximum speed of 397 mph (635 km/hr), and an ordnance load of up to 12,000 lb (5440 kg), giving a gross weight of 43,370 lb (19,670 kg).

The Douglas A-26B Invader had eight 12.7 mm machine guns in the nose and a bombload of 4000 lb (1815 kg). (Harry Gann, McDonnell Douglas)

Other piston-engined attack aircraft from the early postwar period included Britain's Hawker Sea Fury and the twin-engined de Havilland Hornet fighter-bombers. Naval examples included the Westland Wyvern (later turboprop-powered) and the **Douglas A-1 Skyraider** of the US Navy.

The Skyraider was basically a single-seater, designed for dive-bombing and torpedo attacks. It flew in March 1945 and deliveries began in 1947. One of the later variants was the A-1H (originally AD-6), which served with the USN, USMC, and the Vietnam Air Force. It had a 2700 hp Wright R-3350 radial and a maximum speed of 365 mph (585 km/hr). The A-1H had four 20 mm cannon and could carry

A B-26C of the Fuerza Aérea Peruana, *waiting disposal at Las Palmas AB outside Lima in 1974. (Roy Braybrook)*

34

The Westland Wyvern bridged the gap between piston and turbine engines. This pre-production example (VR137) had the R-R Eagle 24-cylinder R.Ea.2SM, but the series aircraft had the Armstrong Siddeley Python turboprop. (Roy Braybrook)

The A-1H was the most widely-used variant of Skyraider in the VNAF. This aircraft (serial 137502) is identified by its 'K' tail-code as allocated to the 518th Fighter Sqn at Bien Hoa. (Norm Taylor, via Robert F Dorr)

8000 lb (3628 kg) externally, giving a gross weight of 25,000 lb (11,340 kg).

During WWII combat aircraft had progressed quickly, since the principals spent however much was needed to develop quickly whatever was required to win. That conflict was followed by a succession of localised wars, many of which were too short in duration for aircraft to be developed to meet new needs as they arose, and in all of which funding was limited. Some of these cases nonetheless taught operational lessons that were incorporated in later air force requirements, and they consequently provide a significant historical background to today's attack aircraft.

The first important conflict occurred in Indo-China, when French forces returned. Outposts were attacked by Communist insurgents, and various aircraft were employed against them, including the Grumman F8F Bearcat and F6F Hellcat, the Spitfire IX, Bell P-163 Kingcobra, B-26 Invader, and the F4U Corsair.

Bearcats supplied to France for use in Indo-China were designated F8F-1D. This example (serial 5492) is armed with HVARs. (Musée de l'Air).

This war came to an end following the French defeat in a pitched battle at Dien Bien Phu in May 1954, which led to the Geneva Accords, the withdrawal of French forces, and the establishment of two Vietnamese states divided by the 17th Parallel.

Beginning in 1948, Britain had its own colonial war to deal with, as Malayan Communists tried to win control. The Malayan Emergency lasted 12 years, and it remains one of the few COIN operations to have been successfully concluded. A remarkable mix of aircraft were thrown into action, from Spitfires and Tempests to RAF and RAAF Lincolns, each of which dropped 14 1000 lb (454 kg) bombs, and even Sunderland flying-boats, each with 360 20 lb (9 kg) anti-personnel bombs.

Beaufighters were replaced briefly by Brigands, then Hornets and finally Venoms. The Lincoln was eventually superseded by the Canberra jet, though at a significant and deplored loss in bombload and endurance. Most of the strikes were carried out in dense jungle, hence target-marking was essential, Austers using phosphorus grenades, smoke or flares.

Though out of Indo-China, the French now had their own COIN war in Algeria, where (despite less vegetation) there were still problems with visual

One of the most useful aircraft for the COIN war in Algeria was the North American T-28D, modified to Fennec standard by Sud-Aviation. This example (51-3690) was photographed in transit through Blackbushe from Morocco to the US in 1978. It had the Sud Aviation c/n 42 and acquired the US registration N54612. (Roy Braybrook)

target acquisition. Progressively slower aircraft were therefore employed. Ouragan jets being superseded by T-28 Fennecs and A-1 Skyraiders, and finally by armed helicopters, Alouette IIs being used with the SS.10/11 wire-guided missile against gun emplacements. At that stage (ie, prior to the advent of man-portable SAMs) the best fixed-wing COIN aircraft were undoubtedly the A-1 and the B-26, though shortages led to the use of other piston-engined aircraft. The **North American T-28D Fennec** was a Sud-Aviation-converted USAF/USN trainer with a 1425 hp Wright R-1820 radial, four underwing pylons, a gross weight of 8250 lb (3740 kg) and a maximum speed of 352 mph (563 km/hr).

In contrast to the COIN wars, the Korean War (June 1950-July 1953) was more conventional, with worthwhile targets such as tanks, bridges, and even power

The RN Historic Flight's Sea Fury FB11 (serial TF956), about to shut down at RNAS Yeovilton in 1982. (Roy Braybrook)

stations, factories and airfields, all easily seen from the air. The North made limited use of the Il-10 (which had begun to replace the Il-2 in Russian service in February 1945) and the Tupolev Tu-2 twin-engined light bomber. The USAF flew ground attack sorties with the B-26, F-51, F-80C, F-84, and even the F-86, while the USN and USMC flew the Skyraider, Corsair and Panther. The RN flew the Sea Fury and Firefly, and the RAAF the Gloster Meteor F8.

Jets had played little part in WWII, hence Korea was more of a transitional war from pistons to turbines. The performance advance is well illustrated by the **Sea Fury** and Meteor F8. The former was the ultimate Hawker piston fighter-bomber, with a 2480 hp Centaurus radial and a maximum speed of 460 mph (735 km/hr). It had a gross weight of 12,500 lb (5670 kg), and was armed with four 20 mm Hispano cannon and 12 RPs or two 1000 lb (454 kg) bombs. The **Meteor** was similarly armed (though it took 16 RPs), but grossed 19,100 lb (8660 kg) and with two 3600 lb (1630 kg) R-R Derwents could reach 512 knots or 590 mph (944 km/hr). Since military operators switched from mph to knots roughly in line with the introduction of jets, that convention is followed in this book.

The **Sea Hawk** used at Suez in 1956 was lighter and slightly faster, the FGA6 reaching 520 knots (964 km/hr) on its single 5200 lb (2360 kg) R-R Nene. Gross weight was 16,153 lb (7325 kg), and it was armed with four 20 mm canon and up to 20 RPs.

With hindsight, technology was lagging behind operational demands in all the 1950s conflicts. The COIN wars would have been best suited to turbo-prop aircraft, combining speed, manoeuvrability and short-field performance, and armoured against small arms strikes. Jungle actions such as Malaya showed the need for attack helicopters, but the turboshaft engines required were not yet available. In contrast, Korea demanded fast jet-powered attack aircraft, as later instanced by the Douglas A-4 Skyhawk, but designers concentrated on the fighter requirements generated by the advent of the MiG-15.

The 1960s brought a fresh series of conflicts of varying importance. The short Indo-Pakistan war of 1965 (like that of 1971) threw little fresh light on air-to-ground operations, and Britain's 1964-67 COIN war in the Radfan (near Aden) mainly reinforced the case for a highly manoeuvrable ground attack aircraft such as the **Hawker Hunter.** It was, however, noteworthy that the Hunter was limited to daylight operation, the attack role at night being taken over by Shackleton patrol aircraft.

Though limited in internal fuel (and thus obliged to carry tanks on two external stations), the Hunter was a good aircraft for strafing and RP attacks. The RAF's FGA9 had a 10,150 lb (4600 kg) R-R Avon turbojet and a clean maximum of over 600 knots (1110 km/hr) at sea level. Maximum weight was 24,420 lb (11,076 kg), and it was normally armed with four 30 mm Aden cannon and RPs. Partly due to the service's Middle East commitments (ie, mud fort targets), the RAF had retained the wartime 'drainpipe', though at the long firing ranges required by jets (1000 metres or more) it was highly inaccurate. Only in the mid-1960s did the RAF begin to introduce the much faster and more accurate Matra 68 mm SNEB rocket batteries, the Hunter carrying two 19-round pods in place of 24 3-inch (76 mm) RPs.

Given its long fatigue life, the Hunter can be updated with various armament and system improvements to remain effective for some years, as in the cases of Singapore and Switzerland. On the other hand, the Hunter was always short of warload-radius performance, due to its limited size and small fuel fraction, and there was a real need for an aircraft like the North American F-100 Super Sabre.

June 1967 witnessed the Six-Day War in which Israel carried out pre-emptive strikes against neighbouring Arab states, demonstrating the value of surprise and the flexibility of the Dassault-Breguet Mirage series. One important point illustrated in this conflict was the Israeli preference for a supersonic fighter-bomber (as instanced by the later Kfir and Lavi), capable of a HI-LO sortie including a high-speed cruise at altitude.

Hawker Hunters of the 'Patrouille Swisse' (Militärflugdienst Dübendorf)

One of the best postwar fighter-bombers was the F-100D, exemplified here by a Royal Danish Air Force aircraft (serial G-779/M) at Greenham Common in 1976. (Roy Braybrook)

The Vietnam War escalated to serious proportions (for the US) in late 1964 and continued until early 1973, with South Vietnam fighting on alone until April 1975. Ground attacks on Communist targets were again flown by a variety of aircraft, few of which were really suitable for the COIN operation in the south. The South Vietnamese Air Force used Bearcats, Skyraiders, T-28D Trojans, F-5As and -5Es, Cessna A-37s and Martin-built B-57B Canberras. American service types used in the south included the A-26 Invader, the F-100, the A-4 Skyhawk, and a series of transport gunships: the AC-47, AC-119, and the AC-130. The RAAF used the Canberra B.20. Target designation was performed by a high-flying 'slow FAC' (forward air controller) in an 0-2 (Cessna 337), OV-10 or C-123, or a low level 'fast FAC' in an F-100 (or other jet), using its speed and manoeuvrability to avoid ground fire.

A VNAF pilot runs for his Northrop F-5A (serial 65-10556). (Northrop Corp)

The **F-100D** was certainly one of the best fighter-bombers of its generation, combining a Mach 1.39 capability at altitude with a useful size and a great deal of fuel. It weighed up to 38,050 lb (17,260 kg) and had a 16,000 lb (7260 kg) P&W J57 afterburning turbojet. It was armed with four 20 mm cannon and up to 6000 lb (2720 kg) of ordnance.

Strikes against the North showed that, having planned for nuclear war, the USAF had no aircraft designed primarily to haul iron bombs over long distances. Initially three-quarters of these sorties were flown by the **Fairchild-Republic F-105,** but with no follow-on production to replace losses the F-105 was withdrawn in stages, leaving the mission to the Guam-based B-52 and the **McDonnell F-4 Phantom II,** the latter having been designed as a naval patrol-interceptor. The US Navy was better equipped for a conventional war, having the **A-4 Skyhawk,** supplemented from 1967 by the Vought A-7 and the all-weather Grumman A-6.

A VNAF pilot stands beside the tail section of his F-5A, its starboard nozzle destroyed by an SA-7 missile. The 'KJ' tail-code indicates that it belonged to the 522nd Fighter Sqn at Bien Hoa AB. (Northrop Corp)

The USAF later adopted a modified A-7, and twice tested the swing-wing General Dynamics F-111A (like the F-105, designed for nuclear strike) in bombing missions against the North in 1968 and 1972.

Leaving aside the development of armed helicopters (discussed later in this book), the Vietnam War was a watershed in attack operations, in the sense that surface-air missiles (SAMs) were employed on a significant scale for the first time. The medium/high altitude SA-2 Guideline was first used successfully in July 1965, and the man-portable SA-7 Grail appeared in 1972. This led to jammer pods and chaff-dispensers on strike aircraft, and dedicated defence-suppression (Wild Weasel) two-seat aircraft, initially the F-100F and later the F-105F.

The real hero of the Vietnam War was the McDonnell Douglas Phantom. This example was an F-4D (serial 56-0644) exhibited at Greenham Common in 1974, at which stage it was based at RAF Lakenheath. (Roy Braybrook)

In the light of COIN demands in the South, the USAF drafted a requirement for a specialised attack aircraft (A-X). It was seen as a short-field, twin-turboprop aircraft with long endurance and a warload that permitted a variety of stores, so that it could attack targets of opportunity. The advent of economical high-bypass turbofans (providing fuel economy at much higher speeds) led to the turboprop concept being abandoned. The subsequent withdrawal from SE Asia changed the emphasis to tank-killing in Europe, which led to the Fairchild A-10 discussed later.

The Vietnam War also brought out the need for single-seaters to be able to

Low-speed aircraft such as the Strikemaster were useful in COIN actions until the advent of the SA-7. This RNZAF example was shown at Le Bourget in 1975. (Roy Braybrook)

operate at low level at night, and the value of 'smart' weapons in attacking heavily-defended hard targets such as bridges. The TV-guided naval Walleye was introduced in 1967, and the laser-guided bomb (LGB) in 1972. In the first three months, LGBs destroyed 106 bridges.

The threat of modern air defence systems was emphasised by the 1973 Yom Kippur War, when Israeli aircraft suffered heavy losses in blunting armoured thrusts by Syrian and Egyptian forces. The COIN war in Oman, which peaked in 1975, illustrated the lethality of the SA-7 against low-speed aircraft such as the Strikemaster, whereas a faster aircraft such as the Hunter could operate with relatively little risk. The SA-7 also appeared in 1978 during the Rhodesian COIN war (1972-79), but again only slow aircraft were shot down, Hunters generally staying above the missile's critical speed of 420 knots (780 km/hr) or above 15,000 ft (4600 m).

Although not part of a proper war, the Israeli strike on 7 June 1981 against Iraq's Tammuz nuclear reactor near Baghdad did serve to illustrate the effectiveness of a modern fighter-bomber. According to press reports, eight **General Dynamics F-16s,** each carrying two 2000 lb (910 kg) bombs, flew this mission from Etzian airfield in south Sinai over a radius in excess of 550 nm (1000 km). Top cover was provided by six F-15s. After the raid, the Iraqis put up barrage balloons to deter further attacks.

The Falklands/Malvinas conflict of 1982 demonstrated the operational flexibility of the British Aerospace Harrier V/STOL series, which operated in both the attack and air defence roles from carriers, shipboard helicopter pads, and an 850 ft (260 m) strip of aluminium planking. The conflict also showed the effectiveness of air-launched anti-ship missiles, not only the Super Etendard-launched Exocet against the destroyer HMS *Sheffield* and the container ship *Atlantic Conveyor,* but also the much smaller Lynx-launched Sea Skua against

patrol boats. Limited but effective use was made of LGBs against tactical targets. The ageing A-4 was found to be still a serious threat to shipping, even with 'dumb' bombs. Other lessons included the urgent need for effective standoff attack weapons against airfields, the need for chaff/flare dispensers on all attack aircraft, and the need for better tactical air-ground communications and improved ground control for CAS attacks.

In the Gulf War between Iran and Iraq (1980-1988) relatively little use was made of Iraq's superior airpower in ground attacks, though the effectiveness of anti-ship missiles (mainly the Exocet) has again been demonstrated. Such strikes included an accidental attack by an Iraqi Mirage F1EQ on 17 May 1987. Two Exocets hit the USN frigate *Stark* and, though only one exploded, substantial damage was caused and 37 men died.

As demonstrated by the Gulf War, the combination of the Mirage F1EQ and the Exocet anti-ship missile was highly effective. (Aérospatiale)

The equally long-running Afghanistan COIN war proved that the Mujihadeen could make effective use of the GD FIM-92A Stinger man-portable SAM. This lightweight IR-homing missile restricted the use of attack helicopters and Su-25 Frogfoots to less well defended areas, and forced high-speed fighter-bombers to make single passes dispensing flares.

There were two technically interesting attack missions in the course of 1986. On February 16 French Air Force Jaguars, escorted by Mirage F1s and supported by C-135F tankers, made an attack on the airfield at Ouadi Doum in northern Chad using Thomson-Brandt BAP100 runway-piercing bombs. This was probably the first operational use of modern runway attack weapons developed for low level delivery, but the airfield resumed full operational use only nine days later.

Equally significant were the Operation El Dorado Canyon night strikes by USAF and USN aircraft against Libyan targets on 15 April 1986. The F-111Fs and A-6Es first identified their targets at long range by radar, then used FLIR (and laser ranging in the case of the F-111F) for precise weapon delivery. Only one aircraft was lost (possibly due to pilot disorientation), illustrating the value of modern avionics in making low level attacks against heavily-defended targets.

Chapter 2 Close Support Aircraft

IN BRITISH PARLANCE, offensive air support for ground forces takes two principal forms: close air support (CAS) and battlefield air interdiction (BAI). The distinction is that CAS means attacks in close proximity to friendly forces, while BAI means more distant operations to disrupt the movement and resupply of enemy forces in the area, and to destroy or temporarily neutralise the enemy's military potential. These two actions are sometimes distinguished by a 'bomb-line', on the near side of which army approval is required for air attacks.

It follows that CAS demands close integration with ground force operations, so that there is no misunderstanding over the target location or the allegiance of the aircraft, and no 'friendly' artillery shells or mortar bombs contesting the airspace.

In essence, CAS supplements or replaces the support normally provided by the army's own mortars, rocket-launchers and artillery. Such firepower may be more sustainable, but it is more restricted than aircraft in mobility and range. Ground weapons have only limited ability to respond to surprise large-scale attacks, and to cope with difficult terrain. Aircraft can easily switch their attacks from one part of the battlefront to another, are less affected by the nature of the country, and are particularly good in responding to an enemy breakthrough and in supporting airborne or seaborne landings, in which organic firepower may be limited initially to light weapons.

In an amphibious landing, naval gunfire can soften up the area in advance, though it is generally inaccurate. Once the marines are ashore, supporting gunfire would probably be directed 1500 metres further inland for safety, gradually reducing to perhaps 500 metres as the fall of shot is observed. In contrast, fixed-wing aircraft in clear conditions can safely deliver bombs within 150 metres of dug-in friendly troops, and can probably strafe within 50 metres, though the safety margins naturally vary according to the service and the circumstances.

On the other hand, air support is expensive, and in the past it has not competed with ground/seaborne weapons in night and bad weather operations. It has sometimes caused unwelcome problems for the people on the ground in terms of craters and rubble. It may also be noted that the recent development of effective low level air defence systems (LLADS) for front-line use is tending to reduce the cost-effectiveness of the manned CAS aircraft.

Close integration between air and ground demands excellent radio communications, though their attainment is an on-going problem. This was certainly a headache for British forces as recently as the Falklands conflict of 1982, despite the absence of Argentine jamming.

Another unsolved problem is that of the CAS pilot in visually acquiring a ground target. Under good conditions a tank may be seen at around 3 km, but haze and the smoke of battle can significantly reduce acquisition distance. A stationary vehicle at the side of a wood may be invisible beyond a few hundred metres, giving the pilot insufficient time to bring his weapons to bear. To facilitate target acquisition and ensure safety for 'friendlies' nearby, CAS normally relies on a forward air controller (FAC) to literally talk the pilot to the aiming-point.

Procedures have varied with nationality and timescale, but the setpiece RAF attack developed for the Hunter and Phantom consisted of a dive over a high-visibility ground panel (near the FAC) toward a target 600-3000 metres distant. The panel was normally a 'T' pointing at the target, and placed out of the enemy's view. Using UHF radio, the FAC would establish an approach path for the aircraft from a sore-thumb initial point (IP), a pull-up point at the end of a timed run, and a turn-point that would take the aircraft over the panel and heading toward the target. When this 'canned' attack was impossible, the FAC would simply give target co-ordinates relative to some convenient reference point.

There are, however, several basic problems in FAC-assisted CAS. The task of the controllers is a highly skilled one, so there are never enough of them, and they are not always in the right place. Since the FAC needs to see the aircraft, the enemy can see it as well, hence the probability of attrition is increased. In addition, communications jamming is standard Warsaw Pact practice, so the FAC may well be unable to function properly.

On the other hand, the advent of lasers in the 1960s brought fresh possibilities to CAS. The target can be 'designated' by a laser aimed by a relatively unskilled observer (on the ground or airborne), and the laser transmission may be coded to avoid confusion between different targets.

If the aircraft has a laser-spot seeker, the target can then be acquired automatically and shown by a marker on the head-up display (HUD). In addition, the aircraft's laser-seeker can be combined with a laser-ranger, giving a precise slant range. 'Dumb' weapons can thus be delivered very accurately.

Thirdly, laser-designation of the target allows it to be attacked even more accurately with a laser-guided bomb (LGB) or a homing missile, possibly released from behind a hill or outside the range of target defences. An LGB is dropped or tossed in the general direction of the target, and in the latter case it is important that the target is not designated too early. This would initiate homing before the bomb's trajectory had peaked, possibly causing it to fall short of the target.

Unfortunately, this category of lasers has introduced new problems in training and exercises, due to the risk of eye injuries to ground personnel. Furthermore, it is debatable whether this (or other advanced forms of weapon delivery) allows attacks closer to friendly troops, since system failures can produce large miss distances. Wartime experience with laser-guided weaponry in the CAS role is still limited.

Operational Requirements

A close support aircraft needs manoeuvrability, protection from small arms fire, a good field of view down over the nose and to the sides, a worthwhile armament (including cannon), and a laser seeker/ranger. Ideally, such aircraft should be equipped for fairly low level operation at night and in adverse weather, though this has only recently become possible.

It should also be able to operate from short strips to achieve quick reaction times from forward sites. The CAS aircraft may not need a long radius of action, though (in a suitable environment) long endurance may be required for airborne 'cab-rank' operations, especially if its airfield performance does not allow 'ground loiter' at small forward strips.

'Cab-ranks' date from Typhoon operations in Normandy, but they were also used by USMC A-4s over South Vietman, taking advantage of a relatively permissive environment. The USAF regarded this as a 'loiter-and-jettison' technique, preferring to respond to US Army demands by diverting preplanned missions. This gave a slower response, though it was argued that this was no longer than the time taken to call off the artillery, etc, and mark the target.

The cruise and attack speeds required depend critically on the air defence environment. The advent of the IR-homing SA-7 in South Vietnam in 1972 brought demands for speeds above 420 knots (780 km/hr) or heights above 15,000 ft (4600 m). The spread of the man-portable SAM has fortunately been a slow process, and there are still important regions where dissidents do not have access to such weapons. In such areas the economic argument in favour of low-performance CAS aircraft is currently overwhelming, especially as they *may* remain viable indefinitely, given the right tactics and chaff/flare dispensers.

Weapons such as rocket projectiles (RPs) can be added to the lightest of aircraft – even microlights – and in a surprise attack in a permissive air defence environment such systems can cause damage out of all proportion to their cost. For example, the Swedish-built 200 hp MFI-17 was reportedly used successfully during Nigeria's war with Biafra in the 1960s.

Nonetheless, in a general sense light aircraft cannot be regarded as serious attack vehicles. Some lower limit must be set in the context of regular close support operations against insurgents armed with only rifle-calibre weapons, and this author would argue that a realistic minimum standard is a 550 shp turboprop aircraft such as the Pilatus PC-7.

Turboprops

The use of an aircraft such as the PC-7 in the close support role is particularly attractive to smaller services in terms of commonality with their trainers, but warload-radius performance is naturally limited. If a turboprop aircraft is designed from the outset specifically for the close support role in a COIN environment, then a much larger twin-engined project can be much more effective and survivable than any trainer. Pilatus was widely expected to develop a twin-PT6-engined attack aircraft named the Mosquito, following the highly successful PC-7 trainer, but instead produced the single-engined PC-9, which is sold as a trainer.

Having the 1150 shp P&WC PT6A-62 flat-rated at 950 shp, the PC-9 is felt by some observers to be overpowered and unnecessarily expensive for the basic flying training role. Similar comments could be made of the Embraer/Shorts Tucano with the Garrett TPE331-12B of 1100 shp. With maximum low level speeds of 268 knots (497 km/hr), both the PC-9 and Garrett-Tucano have worthwhile operational potential. A 1000 lb (450 kg) load can be carried over a maximum radius of around 400 nm (750 km).

The twin-turboprop attack aircraft concept was studied by the USAF in the late 1960s, but abandoned as high-bypass turbofans became available, combining similar loiter performance with higher dash speeds. The US had nonetheless earlier developed a twin-turboprop close support aircraft, the **Rockwell OV-10 Bronco**, though it is used primarily for FAC duties.

This USAF OV-10A Bronco (68-3805) from the 20th TASS of the 601st TCW at Sembach in Germany was photographed at RAF Woodbridge in 1976. (Roy Braybrook)

The OV-10 derives from a 1961 USMC study of a light attack and observation aircraft for COIN wars. The concept gained support from DoD, where it was also viewed as a possible Military Assistance Program (MAP) replacement for the T-6 Texan and T-28 Trojan in COIN duties. In 1964 the North American NA-300 was selected for development.

The resulting OV-10 is a twin-boom multi-role aircraft, normally powered by two Garrett T76 turboprops. It has a two-seat tandem cockpit, and the rear fuselage forms a cargo bay with a capacity of 3200 lb (1450 kg), five paratroops or six infantrymen. Armament is carried on seven stations: two under the wings, one of the fuselage centre-line, and four on 'sponsons' that house four 7.62 mm M60C machine guns. Short field performance is helped by reversible-pitch propellers and two-slot flaps that deflect the slipstream. Roll control is augmented by eight circular-arc spoilers in the upper wing surface. The undercarriage is designed for a 20ft ft/sec (6.1 m/sec) sink-rate at touchdown, to suit operations from rough surfaces. Other useful features include self-sealing tanks, duplicated flying control circuits, and 300 lb (136 kg) of armour. The USAF and USMC versions both have UHF-AM, VHF-FM and HF-SSB radios, and the former variant also has VHF-AM.

Maiden flight took place on 16 July 1965, and deliveries to both US operators began in February 1968. Production orders amounted to 157 for the USAF and 114 for the USMC, and of these around 75 and 45 respectively are still in use today. Both services use the OV-10 in the FAC role, though their operating concepts differ. The USAF aircraft is normally flown as a single-seater by an experienced fighter pilot, orbiting at medium altitude to rendezvous with the attack aircraft, then diving to mark the target with a 2.75-inch (70 mm) FFAR. The USMC operates the OV-10 (like the much faster OA-4M Skyhawk) as a two-seater with a naval aerial observer (a Marine ground officer trained in controlling support fire) in the rear seat. Targets can be marked with the 5-inch (127 mm) HVAR 'Zuni', giving a longer standoff range and a more visible aiming-point. The USMC version differs in having AIM-9s on the wing pylons, a radar-warning receiver (RWR), and ECM provisions. The Marine pilots are trained in defensive air combat manoeuvres (ACM).

The first USMC OV-10As arrived in Vietnam in July 1968. Marine Observation Sqn VMO-2 being attached to the 1st Marine Air Wing at Marble Mountain, near Da Nang. Broncos of the USAF arrived later that month, and were assigned to the 19th Tactical Air Support Sqn (and subsequently the 20th and 23rd TAS) of the 504th TAS Group at Bien Hoa near Saigon. A second USMC unit in Vietnam, VMO-6, was equipped later in the year, and OV-10s later went to one active and two reserve squadrons in the US. Based on outstanding Marine experience with the aircraft, the US Navy acquired 18 from the USMC in 1969 for use by VA(L)-4 'Black Ponies' in supporting riverine patrols in the Mekong Delta.

The Navy Broncos were normally equipped with a centre-line 20 mm gunpod, 7.62 mm Minigun pods and HVARs on the sponsons, and a 10-round pod of FFARs on either wing station. The USAF aircraft were intended purely for the unarmed FAC role, but a mid-1969 'Misty-Bronco' trials programme with six rocket-armed OV-10s gave response times around five minutes, compared to 50 minutes for other tactical aircraft. All USAF OV-10s were subsequently flown with the built-in machine guns and external rockets. Some were converted by LTV for the 'Pave Nail' (night FAC) role, operating as two-seaters with Loran navigation, a Martin-Orlando laser-ranger/designator, and a Varo Inc stabilised night sight.

The OV-10A was followed on the production line by 12 OV-10Bs and 6 OV-10B (Z)s for target-towing in West Germany (the 'Z' indicating the addition of a J85 turbojet pod), 40 OV-10Cs for Thailand, 16 OV-10Es for Venezuela, and 16 OV-10Fs for Indonesia. Several of these export customers use the Bronco in the COIN role.

The most advanced Bronco is the OV-10D, to which standard 18 USMC aircraft has been modified for the night observation surveillance (NOS) role. The OV-10D differs from the – 10A in having T76s of 1040 shp in place of 715 shp, a

Texas Instruments AAS-37 FLIR sensor and laser-ranger/designator in a nose turret, droptank provisions in the wing pylons, special paint to reduce IR signature, and IR-suppression measures on the jetpipes. The prototype also had provision for a ventral turret with a three-barrel 20 mm M-197 cannon, but this option was dropped. Normal maximum weight is increased from 12,600 to 14,170 lb (5715 to 6425 kg), and maximum level speed is up from 235 to 250 knots (435 to 463 km/hr).

The only other twin-turboprop light attack aircraft is Argentina's **IA-58 Pucará** (Fortress), a product of FMA (Fábrica Militar de Aviones), which is now part of FAMA (Fábrica Argentina de Materiel Aerospacial). The first prototype (AX-01) flew on 20 August 1969 with two 900 shp Garrett TPE331s, but the Turboméca series offered more power, so the standard powerplant became the 1000 shp Astazou XVIG, although it suffered initially from surge problems at high AOA. Some 42 USMC OV-10As and 14 OV-10Ds are being brought up to 'D-Plus' standard, with improved avionics and extended airframe life.

The Argentine Air Force (FAA) ordered a total of 108 Pucarás, the first production aircraft (A-501) flying on 8 November 1974. In 1976 deliveries began to *Brigada Aérea III* at BAM Reconquista, and later that year COIN operations were begun by that wing's *No 2 Escuadron de Exploration y Ataque.*

The Pucará is a two-seater, designed to survive fire from light automatic weapons. Survivability features include armour plate for the cockpit floor and engine turbines, a bullet-proof windscreen, and self-sealing fuel tanks. Built-in armament consists of two 20 mm Hispano cannon and four 7.62 mm machine guns. Maximum external load is 3300 lb (1500 kg), but the Pucará has only three pylons. The standard aircraft has a maximum take-off weight of 15,000 lb (6800 kg) and a

maximum speed of 270 knots (500 km/hr). It can deliver a 2650 lb (1200 kg) bomb load over a 220 nm (400 km) radius in a LO-LO mission, or 350 nm (650 km) in a HI-LO-HI profile. Tyre pressure is remarkably low at 45 psi (3.17 kg/cm^2).

The FAA is believed to have around 65 Pucarás left, operating with two squadrons of *Brigada III* and one of *Brigada IX* in the south, at BAM Comodoro Rivadavia. In the 1982 conflict with Britain (in which 26 Pucarás were destroyed or surrendered) all operational missions were flown with a single crew member, and some sorties from Argentina used a 66 Imp gal (300 litre) tank in the rear cockpit.

A total of 24 Pucarás from *Grupo 3 de Ataque* (G3A) of Brigada III were based in the Falklands as the *'Escuadron Pucará Malvinas'*, commanded by Mayor Navarro. A third squadron, from G4A of *Brigada IX*, flew a small number of sorties direct from Santa Cruz, which allowed them to take off with maximum load, but gave a mission radius of around 325 nm (600 km). Cruising at 20,000 ft (6100 m) and descending to low level for the last 120 nm (220 km), this gave a

Five Pucarás from Grupo 3 de Ataque *were brought to the UK in 1982 for evaluation and display purposes. This example was probably A-549, on show at RNAS Yeovilton with centreline twin machine gun pod and underwing FFAR pods. (BAe)*

delay of 1 hr 50 min, by which time the briefed target had often disappeared.

The G3A Pucarás on the islands were generally operated from 1300 ft (400 m) wet grass airstrips, which restricted their external loads to two rocket pods or four 260 lb (118 kg) Mk 81 bombs. This may be compared with the Santa Cruz configuration of a centre-line 264 Imp gal (1200 litre) tank and six Mk 81s or four rocket pods. The Falklands squadrons flew a total of 224 sorties against landing craft, helicopters and personnel. Against helicopters they used 19-round FFAR pods, claiming two Scouts, two Sea Kings and two Wasps. Three Pucará pilots had to use their Martin-Baker zero-zero ejection seats, one due to fire from a Sea Harrier, one to a Blowpipe, and one to a Sea Dart. A further aircraft was lost due to groundfire. The short field performance of the Pucará was exploited in dispersing aircraft from Stanley airport to stretches of the road leading to the town, although they had to return to the airfield for arming and refuelling prior to each mission.

Marketing efforts on the Pucará began in 1977, when two (AX-03 and A-507) were shown at Le Bourget. Two years later AX-05 was exhibited there with the designation IA-58B, the 'Bravo' indicating the use of two 30 mm DEFA 553 cannon in place of the old 20 mm Hispanos. In addition, the avionics system was modified to allow VHF, ADF and VOR/ILS to be operated from either cockpit. The IA-58B was not produced in series, though it may well be available for export sales. It is known that one Pucará (AX-O6) was modified to test 1000/1100 shp Garrett TPE331-11 engines, though it has not been shown at Paris. After the 1982 war, at least one Pucará was converted to single-seat IA-58C 'Charlie' standard, with a

The IA-58B with two 30 mm DEFA cannon in place of the old Hispanos was exhibited at Le Bourget in the form of AX-05 in 1979. (Roy Braybrook)

30 mm DEFA 553 in the upper nose, though retaining the two 20 mm and four 7.62 mm guns. It also has provisions for two Matra Magic or 530 air-air missiles, and for two anti-ship missiles, the CITEFA Martin Pescador (Kingfisher). The fuselage station takes two triple-ejection racks (TERs) in tandem.

The Garrett-Pucará or IA-66 which first flew in December 1980, was developed specifically for Venezuela (presumably to give some commonality with the OV-10E), but no sale resulted. The only export order to date came from Uruguay, which received six standard aircraft in 1981 for use in the attack role, replacing AT-6G Texans. The Central African Republic placed a $12 million order in 1983, but cancelled the contract due to financial problems. It is believed that at least 20 Pucarás were placed in store, pending sale. In 1985 it was announced that a batch of 20 (with an option on 40 more) had been sold to a Middle East country (possibly implying Iran or Iraq), though this has never been confirmed.

Gunships

No discussion of propeller-driven close support aircraft would be complete without mention of the transport gunships that were the Vietnam War's equivalent of the WWII Stuka. Like the Ju 87, the AC-series enjoyed a brief period of glory in a permissive environment, then were virtually wiped out by the opposition. Their usefulness is severely limited, but there are still about 10 AC-130Hs operated as the 16th SOS with MAC's 1st Special Operations Wing at Hurlburt Field, and around 10 AC-130As with the AFRES 919th Special Operations Group at Duke Field, also in Florida. The former unit's 16th SOS in fact supplied AC-130Hs to provide protective fire for the US Army Rangers during the invasion of Grenada in October 1983.

The idea of transport gunships arose in 1963, when US advisers in South Vietnam proposed such aircraft as a means to give continuous night-time perimeter security for airbases and villages under attack. Later the concept was extended equally successfully to night interdiction of supplies moving down the 'Ho Chi Minh trails'. It exploited the transport aircraft's long endurance and immense capacity for flares and ammunition, and the ability of an aircraft in a gentle continuous turn to produce a cone of fire against ground targets (from above the reach of small arms). Various aircraft were converted to the gunship role, but the automatic weapons were always installed to fire to the left, to give the pilot-in-charge a clear view of the target.

The first such gunship was the **Douglas AC-47D**. Known as 'Spooky' or 'Puff the Magic Dragon', it entered service in 1965, armed with two or three 7.62 mm GE Miniguns. The AC-47Ds were flown initially by the USAF 4th Air Commando SOS, but in 1969 this unit was deactivated and the 22 remaining aircraft were handed over to the VNAF, which used them to form the 817th Attack Sqn in June that year. The VNAF also received 24 **Fairchild AC-119G 'Shadow'** aircraft to form the 819th Attack Sqn in September 1971, and 12–16 AC-119K 'Stingers' to form the 821st in December 1972, all three units being based at Tan Son Nhut near Saigon.

The AC-119G was armed with four 7.62 mm Miniguns, but increasing return fire forced them to operate higher, and it was found that these guns were ineffective above 4500 ft (1400 m). This problem was solved by the AC-119K,

which added two 20 mm GE M61 Vulcan cannon. The -119K also differed in having a J85 auxiliary turbojet to improve take-off and climb performance.

Continuing the trend to larger aircraft with heavier firepower, the USAF tested in 1967-68 (and immediately deployed) the **Lockheed AC-130A 'Spectre'** with two 7.62 mm Miniguns and four 20 mm M61s. Two of the M61s were later replaced by 40 mm guns. The AC-130A also had armour protection, a searchlight, LLTV and IR sensors, and a laser designator. Under the 'Pave Aegis' programme, the AC-130 was tested with a 105 mm howitzer. This was so successful that it replaced one of the 40 mm guns in the AC-130E. This ultimate gunship series was in 1973 converted to AC-130H standard, with more powerful engines, and in 1978 these aircraft were equipped for flight refuelling. Some 26 AC-119Gs, 26 AC AC-119Ks, 18 AC-130As and 10 AC-130E/Hs had been produced by 1973.

General William Momyer, USAF, head of the 7th Air Force, described the AC-130 as 'the best truck-killing weapon of the war'. By October 1970, AC-130s were killing 9.72 trucks on an average sortie, compared to 2.3 for the B-57G Canberra. Their success continued until 1972, when the SA-7 missile was introduced into South Vietnam, and increasingly effective AAA was encountered. As the gunships were forced higher, even the 20 mm M61 was ineffective, and these aircraft were restricted to less well defended areas. Even there, survival depended on the early detection of missile firings and prompt flare dispensing. The VNAF nonetheless lost seven of its AC-47Ds to ground fire.

Before leaving the subject of the operational use of transports, it may be added that the VNAF used the C-130 as a bomber, men in the cargo area rolling as many as 24 Mk 81 250 lb (113 kg) bombs off the rear loading ramp, as directed by the pilot. The C-130 was also employed to drop 46 Imp gal (208 litre) firebombs under ground radar control.

It is of some historical interest that C-130s were employed by the USAF (and from 1973 by the VNAF) to deliver over SE Asia bombs that were too large and heavy for normal combat aircraft. These weapons were used initially to clear helicopter landing zones in the rain forests, which were often 300 ft (90 m high, but success in this role led to attacks on troop concentrations. The first bomb was the obsolete 10,000 lb (4535 kg) M-121 developed for the B-36, but as stocks ran out a new 15,000 lb (6800 kg) bomb was manufactured. It was designated BLU-82, and was filled with a mixture of propane and TNT, presumably giving a fuel-air explosive (FAE) effect. As in the case of B-52 attacks, the release of these big bombs was controlled by Skyspot ground radars. The weapon was lashed to a cargo pallet, extracted by parachute from the hold, then released by static-line-activated knives from the webbing that held it on the pallet. It was detonated by a 3 ft (0.9 m) tree-penetration fuze.

The Argentines were later (on 19 May 1982) to use the C-130 as a naval attack aircraft, dropping a stick of eight Mk 82s at a supply tanker, the *British Wye*. All missed except one, which fortunately bounced off the foredeck without exploding. An earlier 'bomber' was the CBU-armed 'Black Spot' NC-123K Provider, first used in Korea.

Despite their limitations, the USAF evidently has no plans to phase out the AC-130. The 10 old AC-130As will be replaced in the early 1990s by 12 new-build AC-130Us, and the 10 existing AC-130Hs are to be updated by Lockheed Aircraft

This photograph taken during the aerial refuelling of a Lockheed AC-130H (serial 69-6577, c/n 4352) shows the radome of the side-looking fire control radar, the air blast deflector for the forward 20 mm Vulcan, and the barrels of the 40 mm Bofors and 105 mm howitzer. (Lockheed Aircraft Corp)

Service Co with TV cameras, IT sensors, new displays and mission computers.

The new aircraft will be built as C-130Hs by Lockheed-Georgia, then converted to AC-130U gunships by Rockwell International. The AC-130U is to be armed with one 25 mm GAU-12/U cannon (as used on the AV-8B), one 40 mm gun, and one 105 mm howitzer. It is to be pressurised and air conditioned to enhance crew effectiveness during long ferry flights and in hot climates. Existing armour is to be superseded by the latest advanced composite protection, saving approximately 2000 lb (900 kg).

Target engagements will be directed by a fire control officer in an armoured, soundproof five-man battle management centre in the mid-cabin section. The AC-130U will be the first gunship with a fire control radar: a modified Hughes APG-70 (from the F-15C/D/E) with its antenna on the left side of the front fuselage. At time of writing, Rockwell has an R&D contract covering the first aircraft, and the USAF has requested the first six production airframes in the FY89 budget.

Light Attack Jets

The operational scope for propeller-driven close support aircraft is decreasing as air defences improve, hence the market is swinging to jets. Dedicated light attack aircraft such as the Fiat/Aeritalia G.91R and small dual-role combat aircraft such as the Northrop F-5A and HAL Ajeet have almost disappeared (notwithstanding the IAR-93/Orao discussed later). The modern trend is toward light attack derivatives of jet trainers, since this reduces development and production costs, and gives equipment commonality.

This Dornier-built Fiat G.91R-3 (serial 32 + 98, c/n 569) was exhibited by the Luftwaffe *at Greenham Common in 1977. (Roy Braybrook)*

For example, the Swedish Air Force employs the Saab 105 (Sk60) in both the flying training and light attack roles, and the German Air Force has used the Alpha Jet for both weapons training and close support, although it is now planned to phase out this latter use. Neither service has used these aircraft in a shooting war, but Israel has employed the Magister operationally, Oman the Strikemaster, and Afghanistan the L-39.

In the 1982 war with Britain, the Argentine Navy deployed six **Aermacchi MB-339As** to Stanley airfield, these being the only jet combat aircraft available that could operate from its 4250 ft (1300 m) runway. The MB-339s were intended to be used in anti-shipping strikes with DEFA 30 mm gunpods and HVARs, though only one such sortie took place (against the frigate *Argonaut*, causing minor damage), their role then being switched to close support. One aircraft undershot the runway, one was destroyed by a Blowpipe SAM, one recovered safely to Argentina, and three with minor damage were abandoned on the airfield. It may

This Swedish Air Force Sk60C is equipped with 30 mm gunpods and a nose-mounted panoramic camera, and can evidently carry large-calibre rockets as an alternative armament.
(I Thuresson, Saab-Scania)

be added that the Argentine Navy also deployed four Beech T-34C-1s, which were based on the 2100 ft (460 m) grass strip at Pebble Island. They flew a few armed reconnaissance missions with 7.62 mm machine guns and seven-round rocket pods before being destroyed on the ground in an SAS raid.

In terms of operational experience, the classic case of a trainer derivative was the **Cessna A-37B Dragonfly**. The prototype T-37 flew in 1954, and 1260 J69-powered T-37A/B/Cs were built, the 'Charlie' having tiptanks, two underwing pylons for weapon training, and increased weight. This T-37C formed the basis for a dedicated attack demonstrator, the YAT-37D, which had J85 engines protected by retractable intake screens, an armoured cockpit, self-sealing tanks, a 7.62 mm GAU-2B/A Minigun in the nose, and six (later eight) underwing pylons.

The first YAT-37D flew in 1963 and was favourably assessed, but the USAF had no immediate need for a light attack aircraft. In little over a year the escalation in Vietnam brought new needs, and in August 1966 Cessna received a contract for 39 A-37As for operational evaluation in SE Asia under the Combat Dragon programme. In the following year the first of 25 A-37As was delivered to the 604th Air Commando (later Special Operations) Sqn, which in four months flew over 5000 sorties from Bien Hoa and Pleiku.

The Cessna A-37B Dragonfly was used effectively by both the USAF and VNAF during the Vietnam War. (USAF photo via Robert F. Dorr)

F-5 VIETNAM COMBAT VETERAN

This is the first F-5 to be withdrawn from Vietnam since the original Skoshi Tiger (4503rd) Squadron of F-5s was formed and entered combat in Vietnam in October, 1965. This airplane has flown 720 combat missions and is back in the U.S. for a series of special tests to be performed in Southeast Asia for the U.S. Air Force. It has flown the 7000-mile journey home from Vietnam. This aircraft is now assigned to the 10th Fighter Commando Squadron and will be returned to active following tests. More than 1000 F-5s have been delivered or are programmed for delivery by the air forces of fifteen nations, including the U.S. which will make it the most widely deployed U.S. fighter aircraft.

The A-37A was criticised only for its short endurance and the limitations on downward view caused by its mid-set wing. The wing position could not be changed, though it is significant that the Fairchild T-46 chosen to replace the T-37 has a high wing. Endurance was increased by means of a flight refuelling probe, design load factor was boosted from 5G to 6G, and crew protection was augmented. The result was the A-37B, of which around 500 were built. It has a maximum weight of 15,000 lb (6800 kg), and two 2850 lb (1290 kg) J85-GE-17As, giving a maximum speed of 440 knots (815 km/hr). In addition to the Minigun it can take 5880 lb (2667 kg) of ordnance on eight stations.

Aside from the A-37s operated by USAF Special Operations units in Vietnam, some 248 A-37A/Bs were given to the VNAF to form 10 squadrons (the 516th, 520th, 524th, 526th, 528th, 532nd, 534th, 536th, 548th and 550th Fighter Sqn). The first was the 524th, which received 20 A-37As in April 1969. The VNAF assessed the A-37 as much more suitable for the attack role than the F-5A, which it had been given in 1967 (initially 20-25 F-5A/Bs, and in the early 1970s around 140 F-5A/Bs and reportedly 126 F-5E/Fs). The gift of F-5A/Bs followed the 1965–66 Skoshi Tiger USAF evaluation at Bien Hoa by the 4503rd Sqn and the 10th Fighter Commando Sqn.

By 1972 A-37s of the VNAF were destroying more tanks per sortie than USAF tactical fighters, partly due to the Dragonfly's manoeuvrability and ability to operate under adverse weather. It was also cleared for blind bombing, using the AN/TPB-1 BOBS (Beacon Only Bombing System). Nonetheless, only a few Dragonflies have been retained by the USAF. A 1987 nose-count gave 22 A-37 FAC aircraft with active units and 60 OA-37s with the ANG, compared to 609 T-37s.

Tandem seaters are more suitable as bases for attack derivatives, since they provide a good all-round field of view when flown solo. For example, the Aermacchi MB-339 led rationally to the single-seat **MB-339K**, which has two 30 mm DEFA 553 cannon in the front fuselage and carries up to 4000 lb (1820 kg) on six pylons. It has a maximum weight of 14,000 lb (6350 kg) and is powered by a 4400 lb (1950 kg) Viper 680 turbojet, giving a maximum speed of 486 knots (900 km/hr).

The single-seat **BAe Hawk 200** is a much larger aircraft with a more economical turbofan, but it is around 50 per cent more expensive. Maximum weight is 20,100 lb (9115 kg), and its 5850 lb (2653 kg) R-R Adour 871 provides a maximum speed of 560 knots (1040 km/hr). It has two very advanced 25 mm Aden cannon mounted internally, and can carry up to 7700 lb (3500 kg) on seven stations.

The **IAR-93B Orao 2 (Eagle)**, jointly developed by Yugoslavia's SOKO and Romania's CNIAR is a dedicated attack aircraft and somewhat larger than the Hawk, but its radius of action is penalised by the use of afterburning turbojets. It has a maximum weight of 24,690 lb (11,200 kg) and two R-R Viper 633s that give a maximum speed of 626 knots (1160 km/hr). It has a very useful cannon armament of two internal 23 mm GSh-23Ys firing 3500 rd/min each, and up to 6175 lb (2800 kg) of ordnance on five stations. The non-afterburning prototype flew in 1974, but the production version had its maiden flight in October 1983, and is now being built for the air forces of both nations.

The first F-5A to return from Vietnam, where it served with the Skoshi Tiger (4503 Sqn), in October 1965. After tests in the US, this aircraft was due to join the 10th Fighter Commando Sqn and return to action. Note the flight refuelling probe. (Northrop Corp)

The Aermacchi MB-339K, as exhibited at Farnborough with the original teardrop-shaped tiptanks. (Roy Braybrook)

Second prototype of the British Aerospace Hawk 200 (ZH200), with what appear to be ferry tanks, centreline tank, and Sidewinders.
(Geoffrey Lee, BAe)

The SOKO Orao 2 in Yugoslav Air Force markings, as shown at Le Bourget in 1985. (Roy Braybrook)

The Nanchang A-5C at Le Bourget in 1987. (Roy Braybrook)

The only other aircraft in this class is China's **Nanchang A-5 'Fantan'**, derived from the MiG-19. The basic idea seems to have been to adopt lateral intakes to allow a nose radar, and to design a stretched fuselage with increased fuel and a ventral weapons bay. In the event all weapons are carried externally, aside from two single-barrel 23 mm cannon in the wing roots. Maximum external load is 4410 lb (2000 kg).

First flight of the A-5 took place in 1965, and several hundred were built for domestic use and exports to North Korea and Pakistan. The latest variant is the A-5M, developed in collaboration with Aeritalia, which company is responsible for the navigation and attack system. The A-5M has two uprated afterburning Shenyang WP-6A turbojets of 8270 lb (3750 kg) and a maximum speed of Mach 1.2 at altitude or 653 knots (1210 km/hr) at sea level. Maximum weight is 26,455 lb (12,000 kg). The A-5M has two extra pylons, giving a total of 12, although only eight can take bombs.

Post-Vietnam Trends

Operations in South Vietnam in the late 1960s showed the need for an attack aircraft with better airfield performance than conventional fighter-bombers, plus low-speed manoeuvrability, long endurance, and invulnerability to small arms fire. Significantly, the resulting USAF requirement was issued in 1970, before the advent of the SA-7 demonstrated the need for high speeds.

The **Fairchild Republic YA-10A Thunderbolt** II first flew on 10 May 1972, a month after the SA-2 and SA-7 appeared in South Vietnam. In January 1973 it was selected in preference to the Northrop YA-9A, and ordered into production. The first unit – the 356th TFS at Myrtle Beach AFB, South Carolina – reached initial operational capability (IOC) in October 1977. The first A-10As began arriving in the UK to form the six-squadron, 108-aircraft 81st TFW at Bentwaters/Woodbridge in 1979. In the event of war in Europe, the 81st would operate from six forward operating locations (FOLs) in Germany. The A-10A also flies from many US bases including Eielson AFB in Alaska, and from Suwon AB in South Korea. The 713th and last A-10A was delivered in March 1984.

The A-10A is a single-seater with two 9065 lb (4110 kg) TF34-GE-100 turbofans, a maximum weight of 50,000 lb (22,675 kg) and a maximum speed of only 368 knots (682 km/hr). It is armed with a massive seven-barrel 30 mm GAU-8/A cannon, which is 21 ft (6.4 m) long and weighs 4190 lb (1900 kg) with 1350 rounds of API ammunition. A normal attack load consists of 1174 rounds plus four Maverick missiles or six Rockeye CBUs or 'Snakeye' retarded bombs. Maximum ordnance load is 16,000 lb (7255 kg) on 11 stations (some units have removed two pylons to improve performance), though full internal fuel reduces this load to 14,340 lb (6500 kg). The recoil from the gun produces a retardation of around 3 knots (5.6 km/hr) for each second of firing. The gun is claimed to be capable of defeating at least the side and rear armour of Soviet tanks. Computer studies indicate approximately 10 kills per sortie, compared to 2.4 for USAF fighter-bombers.

The controversially low speed of the A-10 results largely from the decision to use a 16 percent thick wing section, its designers having aimed for a 400 knot

The Fairchild A-10 was chosen in preference to the Northrop A-9A, illustrated here by the first prototype (71-1367) making its first landing on 30 May 1972. (Northrop Corp)

The distinctive shape of the Fairchild A-10A first appeared at Farnborough in 1976, this example (75-00264) carrying the 'DM' tail-code of the 355th TFW from Davis Monthan AFB. (Roy Braybrook)

(740 km/hr) capability. Rather than flying fast enough to reduce the chance of being hit by ground fire to an acceptable level, the A-10 philosophy is to survive hits, at least by small arms and 23 mm AAA. It has a total of 2887 lb (1310 kg) of armour, including a 1200 lb (544 kg) titanium 'bathtub' around the pilot. The canopy obviously provides no protection, however, and the A-10 has been criticised as a 'one-mission aeroplane', sitting out the rest of the war, waiting to be repaired.

The GAU-8/A cannon and Kaiser HUD are harmonised at a range of 4000 ft (1200 m), but the gun can be used to 10,000 ft (3000 m), and it is argued that this out-ranges the ZSU-23-4. It is planned that A-10s will operate in pairs for mutual support, and with OH-58 and AH-1 helicopters for flak suppression.

A useful indication of the equipment needed in close support work is provided by that of the A-10A, which now includes: AIM-9L Sidewinders for self-defence (although the LASTE gunsight provides for air-air firings with the GAU-8), the Martin Marietta AAS-35(V) Pave Penny laser-spot seeker, Litton inertial navigation, a Westinghouse ALQ-131 jammer, Tracor ALE-40 chaff/flare dispensers, Litton ALR-69 radar warning receiver (RWR) and Magnavox ARC-164 jam-free communications. Some 250 A-10As have provisions for the Martin Marietta Lantirn (low altitude targeting infrared for night) equipment.

A 1987 survey reported 451 A-10As still serving with active USAF units, 106 with the ANG, and 97 with AFRES squadrons. Some observers regret that the USAF never bought the two-seat A-10B, the production version of the company funded night/adverse weather demonstrator, which first flew in May 1979. Equipped with a Westinghouse WX-50 radar, Texas Instruments AAR-42 FLIR, a General Electric LLTV, Ferranti laser ranger. Honeywell radar altimeter, and taller fins, this version would have had more credibility in darkness and bad visibility than the single-seater has on a clear day.

Lighter, better powered, and thinner in the wing than the A-10, the **Sukhoi Su-25 Frogfoot** first flew on 22 February 1975 and in the 1980s saw active service in Afghanistan. Like the A-10, it has a titanium 'bathtub' to protect the pilot; in fact protective measures represent 7.5 per cent of normal take-off weight. The Su-25 is powered by two 9,925 lb (4,500 kg) R-195 turbojets, which can in emergency be run on diesel fuel and provide a maximum speed of 526 knots (975 km/hr) at sea level. It is armed with a two-barrel 30 mm gun with 250 rounds, and underwing ordnance up to 9,700 lb (4,400 kg). With a normal load of 3,100 lb (1,400 kg) and two tanks, take-off weight is 32,200 lb (14,600 lb). With maximum warload and two droptanks, weight rises to 38,800 lb (17,600 kg), giving a LO-LO radius of 400 nm (750 km), or a HI-HI radius of 675 nm (1,250 km).

The fact that not one export customer was found for the A-10A is a clear indication of its lack of credibility. The USAF now admits that air defences have come a long way since its requirement was drafted. The service evidently wishes to phase out the A-10A from 1991 and replace it with an 'A-16', which would be far less vulnerable to ground fire and would have the speed to penetrate beyond the battle area and carry out the BAI role. The 'OA-10A' would replace most OA-37Bs and OV-10As in the FAC role.

It can, however, be argued that an equally logical replacement would be the **McDonnell Douglas AV-8B Harrier II** V/STOL aircraft, which is already used by

A later photograph of an A-10A, with dark-green paint scheme, Pave Penny laser spot-tracker, Maverick missiles, and the 'MB' tail-code of the 354th TFW at Myrtle Beach AFB. (Fairchild-Republic)

Inset: *One A-10A (73-1664) was converted to two-seat YA-10B standard as a night/adverse weather demonstrator, but there was no production order. (Fairchild-Republic)*

Su-25

the USMC in the close support role. The AV-8B is a vastly improved derivative of the BAe Harrier AV-8A/C flown previously by the Marines. The Harrier was the world's first operational high performance V/STOL aircraft, and it owed its success to the simplicity of its single vectored-thrust R-R Pegasus engine, its moderate jet energy producing only limited ground erosion, and its ability to use all the thrust for STO performance.

The original BAe Harrier (of which 147 were built) entered service with the RAF in 1969, making possible operations from small dispersed road-sites close to the troops. This concept appealed to the USMC, and 110 AV-8As with simplified avionics and AIM-9 provisions were purchased. They entered service in 1971, and were later modified to AV-8C standard. The Spanish Navy bought 13 of the USMC version.

Model of the General Dynamics 'A-16', with ventral 30 mm gunpod and six Maverick missiles. (General Dynamics)

Top inset: *The Warsaw Pact's equivalent of the A-10 is the Sukhoi Su-25 Frogfoot, which has a higher thrust/weight ratio and thinner wings. It is seen here in Czech markings. (Letektvi + Kosmonautica)*

Bottom inset: *The Su-25 Frogfoot, making its public début at the 1989 Paris Airshow. (Roy Braybrook)*

The world's first operational high performance V/STOL aircraft was the BAe Harrier, exemplified here by an RAF GR3 (XZ130) of No 1 (F) Sqn, photographed on an exercise in Norway, with temporary whitewash camouflage. (Peter Scott, Rolls-Royce)

British V/STOL development was concentrated on the Sea Harrier (discussed later), hence progress with the 'Land Harrier' was left to America. The USN funded BAe's licensee, McDonnell Douglas (MDC) to develop an improved V/STOL aircraft to replace all three AV-8C and five A-4M squadrons. The resulting AV-8B differs from its predecessor mainly in having an all-new supercritical wing with considerably more area and fuel volume, yet a reasonably light weight due to the use of composite materials. Composites are also used in the front fuselage, tailplane and rudder. Vertical take-off weight benefits from improved intakes, large central strakes and a cross-dam, while STO weight is increased by the large wing and improved flaps.

The current production engine is the R-R Pegasus 11-21 or F402-RR-406. Its thrust of 21,500 lb (9750 kg) is unchanged from the level attained in 1971, though this version has improved TBO, maintainability and reliability. The Pegasus 11-61 or F402-RR-408 will equip USMC FY89 deliveries providing a thrust of 23,800 lb (10,800 kg) and twice the hot-end life. Maximum (STO) weight for the AV-8B is 31,000 lb (14,060 kg) with an ordnance load of 9200 lb (4175 kg) on seven stations, and a 25 mm GE GAU-12/U cannon under the fuselage. Due to the large, thick wing, maximum speed is reduced from the 635 knots (1177 km/hr) of the original Harrier to 562 knots (1040 km/hr). On the other hand, for a given take-off run, the AV-8B can carry roughly twice the load of the AV-8C for a given radius, or fly twice the radius with the same load.

After flight tests with two converted 'YAV-8Bs' from late 1978, the first FSD AV-8B flew on 5 November 1981, and deliveries to VMAT-203 at MCAS Cherry Point, North Carolina, began in January 1984. The first operational unit was VMA-331, which attained IOC in mid-1986. The initial plan was for 328 aircraft, including 28 two-seaters, but production may end with the FY91 buy, giving a total of 280. In addition, 12 EAV-8Bs are being built for the Spanish Navy and 96 Harrier GR5/7s for the RAF (the GR7 being equipped for night attack). In USMC service, the night attack version with GEC Avionics FLIR and 'Cat's Eyes' NVGs, and Smiths HUD, will be introduced with the 167th AV-8B.

The RAF's **Harrier GR5/7** differs in only minor respects from the AV-8B. It has two extra pylons for Sidewinders, leaving the others free for air-ground ordnance. The GR5/7 also has Martin-Baker ejection seats in place of Stencels, and two 25 mm Aden cannon in place of the GAU-12. The RAF aircraft are assembled in the UK by BAe, which company performs 40 per cent of the airframe work for the RAF and USMC aircraft, and 25 per cent for export airframes. The first RAF unit, (No 1 Sqn at Wittering) formed in late 1988.

Both the AV-8B and the Harrier GR5/7 have inertial navigation and a Hughes angle-rate bombing system (ARBS), which employs a dual-mode tracker combining TV and laser sensors. The ARBS is held on target by TV contrast-lock or laser-spot tracking (if the target is laser-designated), and generates line-of-sight and sightline spin-rate data for the mission computer. This unit produces steering commands for the HUD and calculates a release point, weapon release being either manual or automatic.

The principal development proposed beyond the night attack AV-8B with the Pegasus -408 engine is the Harrier II Plus, a radar-equipped version for air defence and anti-ship strikes. The main potential customer is the USMC, hence the Hughes APG-65 radar is the obvious choice for commonality with the F/A-18. If this programme goes ahead, a development aircraft could fly in 1990, leading to deliveries in 1992. Potential naval markets are believed to exist in Italy and Japan.

A McDonnell Douglas AV-8B Harrier II of the US Marine Corps, making a short take-off from a two-lane road at Camp Lejeune, North Carolina. (McDonnell Douglas Corp)

Left: This manufacturer's photograph of the IA-58 Pucará shows it armed with four pods, each appearing to contain nineteen 70 mm rockets and six 125 kg bombs. (FAMA)

Right: The prototype of the Aermacchi MB-339K Veltro II with the later (cylindrical-type) tip-tanks and six Mk 82 low-drag bombs. (Aermacchi)

The Douglas A-1E Skyraider was one of the greatest of piston-engined attack aircraft. Designated AD-5 prior to 1962, the type first flew on 17 August 1951. This example, serial 133913, is shown in the markings of US Navy attack squadron VA-45, with a centreline fuel tank, 12 HVARs and two very old 500 lb (227 kg) bombs. (Douglas Aircraft)

The Nanchang A-5C Fantan, as presented at Le Bourget in 1987, with two ventral bombs, a pair of seven-round RP pods, two drop tanks, and rails for Matra Magic AAMs. (Roy Braybrook)

Second prototype (ZH200) of the British Aerospace Hawk 200, carrying its maximum warload of seven retarded Mk 83 1000 lb (454 kg) bombs. (Geoffrey Lee, BAe)

The McDonnell Douglas AV-8B
Harrier II is the most advanced
V/STOL aircraft currently in
service. This example bears the
'CG' tail-code of USMC attack
squadron VMA-231, and is shown
on a training mission from the
unit's base at MCAS Cherry
Point, North Carolina, armed with
four Mk 82 Snakeye (retarded)
bombs and two AIM-9L
Sidewinders. (McDonnell Douglas)

The Harrier GR5 version of the
AV-8B differs from the USMC
original in several respects,
including an extra pair of pylons
for Sidewinders. Note the white
intakes, to reduce visual
detection range head-on. (Philip
Boyden, BAe)

This Douglas A-4B Skyhawk of the Argentine Air Force was photographed after the 1982 conflict. The unit badge is that of Grupo 4 de Caza, though at the time of the action this aircraft (serial C-222) operated with G5C from Rio Gallegos. (Michael O'Leary)

A Sepecat Jaguar International 'S' (serial NAF705, temporary UK registration G27-392), the first of a batch for Nigeria, pictured on a pre-delivery test flight fom BAe Warton in January 1984. (British Aerospace)

The first production Italo-Brazilian AMX attack aircraft, serial 5500, making its maiden flight on 12 August 1989. (AMX International)

The potential of the F-16 for night-time ground attack is demonstrated by this aircraft equipped with Martin Marietta Lantirn pods under the fuselage, Hughes AGM-65 Maverick missiles, and 308 Imp gal (1400 litre) tanks. (General Dynamics)

Inset: The 'LN' tail-code of this F-111F (serial 72-1443) indicates that it is from the 48th TFW at RAF Lakenheath. It is dropping a stick of twelve Mk 82 bombs with Loral Systems Ballute retarders, over the Bardenas Reales range in Northern Spain. The bulge under the fuselage is the Ford Aerospace Pave Tack target designation system. (SSgt David Nolan, USAF via Robert F Dorr)

The Panavia Tornado IDS in the paint-scheme of the Royal Saudi Air Force, aircraft 704 in the foreground and 701 leading the formation. (British Aerospace)

These British Aerospace Sea Harrier FRS1s are painted in dark sea grey and bear the winged-fist emblem of No 899 Sqn. The aircraft in the foreground is XZ491 (711) and that in the rear XZ457 (715). Both have Sidewinders on twin-store carriers. (Philip Boyden, BAe)

Above left: This Grumman A-6E Intruder (Serial 155688) was originally built as an A-6A. It bears the toned-down markings of VA-128 'Golden Intruders', based at Whidbey Island NAS, Washington. (Grumman Corporation)

Above right: The 'AA' tail-code of this Grumman EA-6B, a four-seat electronics warfare derivative of the A-6, indicates that it is part of VAQ-137 at Whidbey Island. (Grumman Corporation)

Left: When photographed, this Vought A-7E Corsair II (serial 157589) was assigned to VA-105, based on board the USS Forrestal. (US Navy via Robert F Dorr)

An Aérospatial SA.342M of France's Armée de Terre firing the Euromissile HOT-2 anti-tank guided weapon. (Euromissile)

This Westland Sea King HAS Mk 41 (serial 89 + 70) of the West German Marineflieger is armed with BAe Sea Skua sea-skimming anti-ship missiles. (British Aerospace)

The HAP escort/support version of the new Franco-German helicopter will have an air combat capability, using its 30 mm chin turret and wing-mounted Matra Mistral AAMs. (MBB)

The latest derivative of the Bell Cobra series is the AH-1W SuperCobra for the USMC, illustrated here by aircraft 161022, armed with an M197 three-barrel 20 mm gun turret and TOW launch tubes. (Bell Helicopter Textron)

The Aérospatiale SA.365F Dauphin 2, as developed for the Royal Saudi Navy, with Thomson-CSF Agrion 15 radar and Aérospatiale AS.15TT anti-ship missiles. (Aérospatiale)

85

The HAC/PAH-2 anti-armour version of the Eurocopter project, as it will appear in Bundeswehr colours. (MBB)

The Aérospatiale SA.365M Panther is shown here armed with two 20 mm GIAT cannon pods. (Aérospatiale)

Early production example (serials EI-901 and -903) of the Agusta A.129 Mangusta, from a batch of 60 being built for the Italian Army. (Agusta)

The Bell Model 406CS (Combat Scout), seen here armed with a seven-tube RP pod and a twin machine gun pod, is being produced for Saudi Arabia. (Bell Helicopter Textron)

Above: This McDonnell Douglas Model 500MG Scout Defender of the Kenyan Army is equipped with the same manufacturer's 7.62 mm EX-34 Chain Gun. (McDonnell Douglas Helicopter Co.) Below: The most advanced attack helicopter in the world is the McDonnell Douglas AH-64A Apache, as used by the US Army. Note the underslung 30 mm M230 Chain Gun. (McDonnell Douglas Helicopter Co.) Right: Artist's impression of the McDonnell Douglas/Bell Helicopter Textron LHX light scout/attack helicopter. (McDonnell Douglas Helicopter Co.)

Chapter 3　**Ground Attack Aircraft**

SOME OPERATORS USE the expression 'ground attack' for any type of air-to-ground operation involving non-nuclear weapons. From a designer's viewpoint, ground attack aircraft are products such as the Vought A-7D and Aeritalia/Aermacchi/Embraer AMX, ie, aircraft with the performance (which close support aircraft lack) to penetrate enemy territory and restrict the movement of second echelon forces, but without the long-range capability of the Tornado and F-111 strike fighters.

Due to its need to survive in a sophisticated defence environment, a typical ground attack aircraft is capable of penetrations at speeds in the 500-600 knot (925-1100 km/hr) category and has a moderately high wing loading to restrict gust loads on the airframe and crew members. Likewise its need for a radius of action of 200-500 nm (370-925 km) leads to an aircraft that is significantly heavier than a close support type such as the Alpha Jet, but far lighter than (say) a Tornado. On published figures for equipped empty weight, the 14,770 lb (6700 kg) of AMX is almost twice the weight of the 7750 lb (3515 kg) Alpha Jet, and less than half the weight of the 30,800 lb (14,000 kg) Tornados IDS.

In the 1950s and early 1960s most ground attack sorties were flown at medium levels, with weapons delivered in dives to ensure accuracy. The pilot generally navigated by stopwatch and compass. If he wished to approach the target at low level, he would bias his aircraft's track to one side of the objective, so that in pulling up to sight the aiming point he need search on only one side of the nose.

In the standard RAF Hunter rocket attack about 1960 the aircraft would roll in from around 6000 ft (1850 m), enter a 30-degree dive, and fire at a height of about 1500 ft (450 m) and a speed of 380 knots (700 km/hr). A 6G recovery would then ensure that the aircraft did not pass below the safety height of 800 ft (250 m).

Prior to Vietnam, US aircraft reportedly rolled in from at least 7000-10,000 ft (2150-3050 m), using a 30-45 degree dive, and releasing bombs at 3000-5000 ft (900-1525 m). However, weather restrictions in SE Asia often made these steep dives impractical, hence low angle 10-20 degree bombing was introduced, rolling in at only 4000-5000 ft (1200-1525 m) and releasing at 1500-2500 ft (450-760 m).

In Europe the view has for many years been that the only way to penetrate a modern defensive system is to fly at extremely low level, since this minimises the warning given by surveillance radars and the firing opportunities for air defence

systems. To illustrate the effect of aircraft height on the theoretical acquisition range of a ground radar, a target flying at 30,000 ft (9150 m) may be seen at around 220 nm (400 km), whereas a target at 1000 ft (300 m) may be picked up by a ground level radar at only 40 nm (75 km). In peacetime the limit for RAF low level flying is 250 ft (75 m), but in war pilots would enter air defence envelopes well below 100 ft (30 m).

One of the major drawbacks to low level operation is that the range of the aircraft is reduced to 35-50 per cent of that achieved at altitude. The USAF philosophy is consequently to cruise at medium level, relying on air superiority to minimise losses due to enemy fighters, and on electronic countermeasures to render SAM systems ineffective. It may be that the Soviet Air Force would adopt the same approach, relying on a combination of numbers and technical quality to achieve locally the supremacy that America takes for granted.

Another problem in low level operation is that, just as ground radars have difficulty in detecting the aircraft, the pilot has difficulty in visually acquiring his target. When flying at 100 ft (30 m), the pilot's effective field of view is approximately 1.0 nm (1850 m) in good visibility. At a speed of 600 knots (1110 km/hr) he thus sights the target only 6 seconds prior to overflying it, and an even shorter interval before reaching his release point. If the pilot has to make any significant correction to his aircraft's flight path, then he may well be unable to carry out the attack.

It is obvious from such considerations that a low level ground attack aircraft must have a highly accurate navigation system, otherwise the pilot will miss his checkpoints and the target, or will see the target too late to attack it. It is also clear that when navigating at very low level, to avoid ground impact the pilot must be free to fly head-up continuously, rather than looking down in the cockpit at his instruments. The aircraft thus requires a system that automatically computes its present position and velocity vector, and shows the resulting navigation information (eg, heading instruction and distance-to-go) on a reliable head-up display (HUD), superimposing this navigation data on the pilot's view of the outside world, along with flight instrument displays and weapon-aiming markers.

Accurate dead-reckoning navigation systems came into use in the mid-1960s in the form of the Litton LN-3 inertial navigation system (INS) for the Lockheed F-104G Starfighter, which gave an accuracy of around 2.0 nm/hr (3.7 km/hr). Compared to alternatives based on radio aids and Doppler-compass systems, the INS was not only more accurate, but was immune to countermeasures, did not radiate detectable signals, was completely manoeuvrable, was not saturated by numbers of aircraft, and had effectively no geographic, altitude, weather, or time-of-day limitations.

The traditional INS derives from ballistic missile technology, and has three accelerometers mounted on a stable-table, ie, a gimballed, gyrostabilised platform, which is maintained level and north-pointing. The outputs from the accelerometers are integrated firstly to give velocity components, and again to give position. In the last 20 years small computers have become much more capable, and it has become possible to dispense with the stable-table. The resulting strapdown systems are simpler mechanically, lighter, and far more reliable, increasing MTBF (mean time between failures) from around 300 to 2000

A Royal Navy Hunter GA.11 from the Fleet Requirements and Air Direction Unit (FRADU) firing two-inch (51 mm) rockets during weapons practice. (David O'Brian, HMS Heron)

hours. Another important development is the use of ring laser gyros (RLGs) to measure rotation rates. Modern INS equipment now produces accuracies of around 1.0 nm/hr (1.85 km) in tactical aircraft applications. The INS is here to stay, though another (and even more accurate) form of navigation will be available in the early 1990s.

The big breakthrough is satellite navigation, which offers the prospect of mind-boggling accuracy, though it is debatable whether such a system could be relied upon in a major war. The US Defense Department's Navstar (navigation system time and range) GPS (global positioning system) is an automatic passive ranging system that computes the distance of the user equipment from three or more satellites, which are continually updated with time and position data by ground stations. Each satellite transmits its identification, position and time of transmission on two frequencies. Civil users will have free access to the coarse acquisition (C/A) code, giving a position accuracy of 330 ft (100 m), while approved military users will have access to both the C/A and precision (P) code, giving an accuracy of 52.5 ft (16 m). The P-code will also provide time to an accuracy of 100 nanoseconds, a precision that is essential in the use of frequency-hopping secure radios.

For military users, Navstar GPS will provide an accuracy that will make nonsense of most existing maps, and will make possible the effective delivery of large conventional bombs without the target being seen by the crew or acquired by the sensors of the attacking aircraft. The Navstar system is naturally designed for some degree of survivability in a war between the super-powers, ie to tolerate some loss of satellites and some degree of jamming. Nonetheless, it appears that military aircraft will be equipped with both GPS and a reversionary navigation system such as INS, so that missions can be continued in the event that Navstar is rendered completely inoperable.

At present many other essential items of operational equipment are generally added externally, such as laser designators, chaff/flare dispensers, FLIR, and jammers. This approach is the result of most current combat aircraft having been designed before such equipment became available. It seems reasonable to suppose that future aircraft will carry these items internally, which will result in slightly larger airframes, but will ensure that all external stations are available for weapons (or auxiliary fuel tanks).

Whether ground attack aircraft should have forward-looking radar is increasingly open to question, primarily due to the growing emphasis on reduced detectability or stealth. A radar is undoubtedly useful in detecting a ship, a shoreline target, or other sore-thumb objective such as an oil refinery. However, in a more general ground attack context the real justification for a radar was all-weather terrain following avoidance. Terrain following (TF) means varying height to provide a preselected minimum clearance while on a fixed track, while terrain avoidance (TA) means varying heading to avoid ground rising above the height of the aircraft. Given a precise (1990s-technology) navigation system and accurate knowledge of terrain contours, it is anticipated that it will be practical to operate safely at low level by virtue of terrain-reference navigation (TRN), automatically comparing radar altimeter data with a digitally-stored three-dimensional map of the land overflown. If current expectations for TRN are confirmed, then the case for radar will be considerably weakened.

Modern operational equipment is vitally important if an aircraft is to remain effective in the face of the latest air defence systems, by day and night, and regardless of weather. However, the fundamental challenge in the design of a ground attack aircraft is to reach a good compromise between thrust/weight ratio and fuel fraction. In designing to meet the requirements of the launch customer, the best possible radius of action is achieved by matching the engine precisely to the thrust requirement in the cruise phase, corresponding to aircraft drag with design warload. This results in the smallest possible engine, and hence the highest possible fuel fraction. Unfortunately, other customers may demand to see performance with warloads in the region of 15,000 lb (6800 kg), or with multiple high-drag clusters of small munitions. The minimum engine approach is then liable to show maximum cruise speeds that would make the aircraft a sitting duck.

This design approach also leads to a poor take-off performance. The tendency in the 1960s was to size the engine to meet cruise drag demands, then add afterburner to get the aircraft off the ground in a reasonably short distance, an approach illustrated by the Sepecat Jaguar. However, the fact that the only export customers for the Jaguar have been Ecuador, Oman, Nigeria and India suggests that this 'design-point' philosophy lacks the flexibility needed to achieve large-scale sales.

The classic example of the small dedicated ground attack aircraft is probably the **Douglas A-4 Skyhawk**, which around the time of its first flight in 1954 enjoyed considerable publicity simply for being much smaller and lighter than the US Navy had expected. The early models had the 7700 lb (3490 kg) Curtiss Wright J65, but the Pratt & Whitney 8500 lb (3855 kg) J52-P-6 was introduced with the A-4E, prior to a series of upratings, culminating with the 11,200 lb (5080 kg) J52-P-408 in the Marine Corps' A-4M. Empty weight meanwhile grew from 8400 lb (3810 kg) to 10,465 lb (4745 kg), and maximum gross went up from 20,000 lb (9070 kg) to 24,500 lb (11,110 kg). Internal fuel is approximately 5270 lb (2390 kg). Maximum speed clean is 608 knots (1126 km/hr).

The A-4 established an excellent record for survivability in SE Asia and the Middle East, due to its multi-spar wing construction and manual reversion flight controls. The A-4M has a HI-LO-LO-HI radius of 275 nm (510 km) with a 4000 lb (1815 kg) bomb load, or 460 nm (850 km) with half that load. Production ended in February 1979 with delivery of the 2960th aircraft, which included 555 trainers. The A-4 has served with the forces of nine countries.

At time of writing it is estimated that some 1400 A-4s remain in service. The most advanced of these are the A-4S-1 Super Skyhawks refurbished and re-engined by Singapore Aircraft Industries, using the lighter and more economical General Electric F404-GE-100D turbofan of 10,800 lb (4900 kg) thrust.

For the US Navy the successor to the A-4 was the **Vought A-7 Corsair II**, although the Marine Corps never accepted this much larger aircraft. The new VAL light attack aircraft had to be able to carry a 7500 lb (3400 kg) bombload over a 200 nm (370 km) radius, and it had to be derived from an existing design to minimise R&D risks and costs. The winner, which flew in 1965, was the Vought A-7, a derivative of the supersonic F-8 Crusader.

Line-up of Douglas A-4B Skyhawks, waiting delivery to the *Fuerza Aérea Argentina*. *In the foreground is C-233, followed by C-228 and -235. (Harry Gann, McDonnell Douglas Corp)*

A Royal Malaysian Air Force (TUDM) TA-4PTM, M32-01, one of a batch of 40 ex-USN Skyhawks refurbished and updated by Grumman. (Grumman Corp)

The first aircraft to be modified by Singapore Aircraft Industries to A-4S-1 Super Skyhawk standard (serial 946, presumably the former 646), with General Electric F404 engine. (Singapore Aircraft Industries)

A Vought A-7D (71-0296) of the Pennsylvania ANG, photographed during deployment to RAF Wittering in 1978 as part of Exercise Coronet Teal. (Roy Braybrook)

At the end of 1965 the USAF, well aware that the F-100D did not have the warload-radius performance for strikes into North Vietnam, and that the number of F-105Ds available was strictly limited, decided to adopt a variant of the Navy's A-7 as its next ground attack aircraft.

The first of 459 A-7Ds first flew on 5 April 1968, and deliveries began in September 1970. In October 1972 some 72 A-7Ds of the 354th TFW were deployed to Korat in Thailand, and in the few months left before the US withdrawal these aircraft flew 6848 sorties against the Communists.

The A-7D differs from preceding Navy aircraft in having a 14,500 lb (6577 kg) Allison TF41-A-1 turbofan in place of the TF30 (although the Navy's A-7E also has the TF41), an M61 six-barrel Gatling-type gun in place of the pair of single-barrel Mk 12s (also of 20 mm calibre), and receptacle-type refuelling in place of the Navy's probe. The A-7D has an empty weight of 19,781 lb (8973 kg) and a maximum take-off weight of 42,000 lb (19,050 kg). It has a maximum speed clean of 575 knots (1065 km/hr) at sea level. Internal fuel is approximately 9400 lb (4265 kg).

In a 1987 nose-count active USAF units had only 31 A-7Ds, but ANG squadrons had 342, and AFRES units some 97. The only export A-7s have been naval variants, Greece's 60 A-7Hs and 5 TA-7Hs being new-build aircraft based on the A-7E, and Portugal's 43 A-7Ps and 6 TA-7Ps being refurbished and modified A-7As (with TF30-P-408s).

In 1985 the USAF asked for proposals for an interim CAS/BAI aircraft to supplement the A-10, pending acquisition of the A-16. The A-7 was chosen as the basis for this program, and in 1987 the manufacturer (now known as the LTV Aircraft Products Group) was contracted to modify two ANG A-7Ds to A-7 Plus standard, later to be designated YA-7F. The first was to fly in mid-1989 and, if successful, LTV would then compete to modify around 337 ANG A-7Ds to A-7Fs.

The A-7F will differ in powerplant, operational equipment and in various airframe respects from the A-7D. The YA-7F will fly with an afterburning F100-PW-220 of about 26,000 lb (11,800 kg) thrust, making it marginally supersonic clean at altitude, although the engine bay is designed to take alternatively the F110-GE-100. Its equipment will include LTV's LANA (low

altitude night attack) system, which is currently being retrofitted to 72 ANG A-7Ds and 8 two-seat A-7Ks. It is based on the Texas Instruments AAR-49 FLIR, producing a picture on a wide-angle HUD by GEC Avionics. Airframe modifications include a 47.5-inch (120 cm) fuselage extension to increase space for avionics and fuel, a taller fin and wing strakes to improve handling at high AOA, an automatic manoeuvring flap and a trailing edge flap augmentor, and spoilers to shorten landing distance.

The **Sepecat Jaguar** is a much lighter aircraft than the A-7, and it has two engines, which is reportedly why the Indian Air Force chose it (for better survivability against enemy action and birdstrikes) over the AJ37 Viggen and Mirage F1, in replacing the Hunter and Canberra. The engines are Rolls-Royce/Turboméca Adours, originally the Mk102, each giving an afterburning thrust of 7300 lb (3310 kg), and in the latest export aircraft the Mk811 of 8400 lb (3810 kg). The Jaguar has an empty weight of 15,400 lb (6985 kg), some 7167 lb (3250 kg) of internal fuel, and a maximum take-off weight of 34,620 lb (15,700 kg). In clean configuration it can reach Mach 1.1 at sea level and 1.6 at altitude.

Artist's impression of the A-7F, with modifications that include wing strakes and the afterburning F100 or F110. (LTV Aircraft Products Group)

This French Air Force Jaguar is armed with Matra laser-guided bombs, allowing release at 2.2-5.4 nm (4-10 km) from the target. (Matra)

Two RAF Jaguar GR.1s from No 20 Sqn, based at Bruggen. In the foreground, ZX384/CM, with eight 1000 lb (454 kg) free-fall bombs, and in the background XX959 with two LGBs, a Westinghouse ALQ-101 jammer pod on the port outer pylon and a Phimat chaff dispenser on the starboard outer pylon. (BAe)

The most recent development in the ground attack category is the **Aeritalia/Aermacchi/Embraer AMX**, designed to meet joint Italo-Brazilian requirements, associated with initial needs for 187 and 79 aircraft respectively. The AMX is similar in size to the Jaguar, and around 70 per cent of the weight of the A-7. To minimise development risks and unit cost, it was designed around a single non-afterburning Rolls-Royce Spey Mk807 of 11,030 lb (5000 kg) thrust. It has an empty weight of approximately 14,770 lb (6700 kg) and a maximum take-off weight of 27,500 lb (12,500 kg), although in time this will be increased to 28,665 lb (13,000 kg).

The AMX has a spacious cockpit with an outstanding field of view, especially down over the nose, and an exceptional degree of post-failure operability. Most essential equipment aside from the pilot and the engine is duplicated. Wing

Main pic: *Side-view of AMX in Brazilian Air Force markings. (Embraer)*

Left Inset: *Head-on view of AMX, illustrating the excellent field of view over the nose of the airfraft. (AMX International)*

Right Inset: *The first production AMX, painted light grey to reduce the chance of visual detection from the ground, and with Italian Air Force roundels of reduced size. (Aeritalia)*

loading is somewhat higher than for most of its predecessors in order to reduce gust response, relying on leading- and trailing-edge flaps to ensure reasonable airfield performance and manoeuvrability around 350 knots (650 km/hr).

Maximum clean sea level speed is 550 knots (1020 km/hr), and with external stores the AMX can still achieve a penetration speed of 500 knots (925 km/hr). In a LO-LO mission with eight 500 lb (227 kg) bombs, it has a radius of 220 nm (410 km) on internal fuel. With a pair of 2000 lb (910 kg) bombs and 128 Imp gal (580 litre) tanks it has a HI-LO-LO-HI radius of 500 nm (925 km). With a pair of 1000 lb (454 kg) bombs and two 240 Imp gal (1100 litre) tanks this radius is increased to 720 nm (1335 km). All these figures assume the carriage of two AIM-9 Sidewinders on the wingtips and internal ECM equipment.

One of the most widely-used of Soviet ground attack aircraft is the Sukhoi Su-17 Fitter C, seen here in landing configuration. (US Navy photo, via Robert F Dorr).

The Mirage F1 is a good example of a dual-role combat aircraft, a true replacement for the Hawker Hunter in the export market. (Dassault-Breguet)

Future developments planned include the Fiar Grifo-ASV radar for the anti-shipping role, a more powerful engine, and automatic manoeuvring flaps for the Mach 0.80-0.85 range.

For any major air force there should be no great problem with the concept of buying a dedicated attack aircraft. Having been designed from the outset to excel in this role, it will presumably be more effective and less expensive than any alternative aircraft designed for both the air-to-ground and the air-to-air roles. On the other hand there are also attractions – even for a major air force – in having both its attack and air superiority squadrons equipped with the same basic type. In the case of a small air force it may be essential to limit combat aircraft procurement to a single type, and even to have its pilots trained to some degree of proficiency in both ground attack and air superiority roles.

The dual-role potential of the McDonnell Douglas Eagle (leading to the F-15E) was demonstrated by this F-15B (71-0291) shown at Farnborough in 1980, with Fastpac conformal

Some of the most exportable ground attack aircraft have begun their lives in the air-to-air role. Examples include the Hawker Hunter, Dassult-Breguet Mirage 5, Lockheed F-104G, McDonnell Douglas F-4E, North American F-100D, and the MiG-17 and Su-7/17 family. A particularly good example is the dual-role Mach 2 Mirage F1, which has been exported to 10 countries and has almost as good a warload-radius performance as the single role Jaguar, which has been exported to only four operators. More recent examples of fighter derivatives with good attack capability include the F-16, MiG-27 and F-15E.

fuel tanks and a wide variety of stores. Those visible on the ground include Durandal runway-piercing bombs and the Ford Pave Tack EO/laser pod. (Roy Braybrook).

The feasibility of developing an effective dual-role (or 'swing-force') combat aircraft was one of the more important lessons to emerge in the 1960s and 1970s. This fact is perhaps best illustrated by the visit to Europe by General Dynamics' YF-16 in 1975, with demonstrations that led to a complete about-face in RAF requirements. Previously the Air Staff had been planning a joint Harrier-Jaguar replacement (AST.396) in the form of a subsonic attack aircraft with the V/STOL performance of the Harrier and the warload-radius performance of the Jaguar. When it was found that an air combat fighter could provide virtually the same warload and radius (and almost as smooth a ride) as a dedicated attack aircraft AST.396 was abandoned in favour of a new supersonic concept (AST.403), effectively a V/STOL F/A-18. To complete this story, the V/STOL requirement was dropped when Britain's European partners showed no interest.

Whereas the YF-16 had been designed purely for the dogfight role, the McDonnell Douglas F/A-18 Hornet was developed (from the Northrop YF-17, which had lost the USAF contest to the YF-16) for both the fighter and attack roles, replacing both the US Navy's F-4J and A-7E. The success of the F/A-18 has now inspired the development of two more advanced dual-role aircraft: the Dassault-Breguet Rafale and the Eurofighter EFA.

The F/A-18A Hornet is one of the best dual-role aircraft available, replacing both the F-4J and A-7E in US Navy service. These Marine Corps examples bear the 'VW' tail-code of the first operational Hornet unit, VMFA-314 'The Black Nights', which attained IOC at MCAS El Toro in January 1983. (McDonnell Douglas Corp)

Although artists' impressions of the forthcoming Eurofighter EFA emphasise air combat, it is intended equally for the air-ground role, replacing aircraft such as the Jaguar. (Eurofighter)

Chapter 4   **Strike Aircraft**

FOR THE PURPOSE of this discussion, the term 'strike aircraft' is used to mean those types with the ability to deliver conventional or nuclear weapons over a radius in excess of 500 nm (925 km). Such a radius implies a comparatively large, heavy aircraft with design emphasis on fuel fraction rather than thrust/weight ratio.

Long-range penetration of advanced defences requires day/night all-weather capability and effective operation for extended periods at high speed and low level. Since the associated systems are the most sophisticated in any attack category, there may well be a case for a two-man crew. If the crew is to remain effective and the airframe is not to fatigue, then the design of the aircraft must emphasise reduced gust response. This in turn demands a comparatively high wing loading and a planform of low aspect ratio and high sweep.

In the case of the F-111 and Tornado, the desired result has been achieved though the use of variable sweep, which makes possible a combination of low gust response and moderate airfield performance, though at a significant structural weight penalty. The ill-fated TSR.2 had a tailed-delta configuration, which required a comparatively high thrust/weight ratio to ensure an acceptable take-off performance. The AJ37 Viggen has a modified delta wing, but uses a canard trimming surface. The canard arrangement has an advantage over a traditional aft-tail in airfield performance, since the foreplane produces positive (upward) lift to trim and (in the case of an all-moving foreplane) to rotate the aircraft for unstick.

High penetration speed in the context of the final dash toward the target demands afterburner (the powerplant having been sized for cruise), and it may favour the use of an internal weapons bay. An internal bay is a feature of the F-105, F-111 and Buccaneer, but it has the disadvantage that it is generally suited to only one specific design load. In addition, arranging for stores to depart from an internal bay cleanly may be more difficult then ejecting them downwards from an external pylon.

The leader in the strike category was the **Republic F-105 Thunderchief,** which was designed to deliver nuclear weapons in a HI-LO sortie. It first flew in 1955, entered service in 1958, and could reach Mach 2.10 at altitude. Empty weight was 26,855 lb (12,180 kg) in the case of the standard F-105D, which had a 26,500 lb (12,000 kg) J75-P-19W afterburning turbojet. Normal take-off weight was

35,637 lb (16,165 kg), and maximum gross was 52,840 lb (23,465 kg). Some 833 F-105s were built, including 610 F-105Ds and 143 two-seat F-105F/Gs, which were mainly used as Wild Weasel defence-suppression aircraft in Vietnam. By late 1968 around 400 had been lost, mainly in strikes against North Vietnam. Survivability modifications introduced on the F-105 during that conflict included a tailplane lock (to prevent run-aways), additional armour, ECM pods, the use of differential flap for roll control, self-sealing tanks, foam in the fuel tanks and surrounding cavities, a two-shot fire extinguisher system, a redundant fuel system, and a third hydraulic system.

Throughout the period 1965–68 the main USAF strike force had consisted of two 55-aircraft F-105 wings at Thai bases: the 355th TFW at Takhli and the 388th TFW at Korat. However, in November 1970 the F-105D was withdrawn from SE Asia, by 1972 most of the F-105Gs had been replaced by F-4s, and at the end of October 1974 the 'Thud' was finally withdrawn to the US. The F-105 was probably the largest and most effective single-seat combat aircraft ever to see operational service, and it was described by Gen William W. Momyer (commander of the USAF 7th Air Force) as the finest aircraft to participate in the Vietnam War.

When pictured in 1970, this Republic F-105F Wild Weasel (serial 62-4434, later converted to F-105G standard) had QRC-380 blisters on the sides of the fuselage, and was armed with both the AGM-45 Shrike and the much larger AGM-78 Standard ARM. (USAF photo, via Robert F. Dorr).

The F-105G Wild Weasel, with APR-25 radar warning receiver, APR-26 missile launch warning receiver, ALQ-105 jamming equipment, and provisions for the Shrike and Standard anti-radar missiles, remained in service after the F-105D had been phased out. The 35th TFW at George AFB in California flew its final F-105G sortie in July 1980, the last ANG sortie was flown in May 1983, and the final AFRES sortie in February 1984.

Although the F-105 is no longer in service, it has been considered in some detail because it is the only strike fighter with considerable operational experience, and since it established the pattern for modern defence-suppression aircraft. The F-105 was replaced as a strike fighter in active USAF units by the **General Dynamics F-111** series of far heavier two-seat, swing-wing aircraft. The F-111A had its maiden flight on 21 December 1964 and deliveries began in early 1968 to the 474th TFW. The availability of this aircraft presumably explains why production of the F-105 was terminated in January 1965 and why Republic's proposals to re-open the line in the late 1960s were turned down.

The first F-111 operational trials were carried out in March 1968 by six aircraft (later augmented by two more) from the 428th TFS of the 474th. Based at Takhli in Thailand, the detachment flew 55 single-aircraft missions, mainly subsonic low level night attacks using automatic terrain following. After three aircraft were lost the trial was abandoned, and it was later established that the probable cause was fatigue failures in the tailplane actuators. Some 48 aircraft were deployed from the 429th and 430th TFS (also from the 474th TFW) to SE Asia from September 1972 to March 1973. On this occasion the F-111As flew over 4000 combat missions and suffered only six losses, despite the fact that it operated without the fleet of tanker, defence-suppression, MiG-CAP, chaff-bomber, strike escort and stand-off jammer aircraft that the F-4s required for their attacks. The F-111 had its full share of development problems, but it was the only Western aircraft capable of fulfilling the low level day/night all-weather strike mission, and so it remained until the advent of the Tornado.

A total of 141 F-111As were built, followed by 24 F-111Cs for the RAAF, 96 F-111Ds, 94 F-111Es, 106 F-111Fs, and (for SAC) 76 FB-111As. Some 42 F-111As were subsequently converted by Grumman to EF-111A electronic warfare aircraft. Empty weight grew from 44,948 lb (20,388 kg) in the case of the F-111A to 47,445 lb (21,520 kg) for the FB-111A. With 32,800 lb (14,875 kg) of internal fuel and a dozen 830 lb (375 kg) M117 bombs, the F-111A grosses 92,360 lb (41,885 kg), but maximum take-off weight is 98,850 lb (44,830 kg). The FB-111A has a maximum take-off weight of 116,115 lb (52,660 kg), though with in-flight refuelling it can reach 122,900 lb (55,735 kg).

The F-111A is equipped with two 18,500 lb (8390 kg) TF30-P-3 afterburning turbofans, and the most powerful of the series is the F-111F with 25,100 lb (11,385 kg) TF30-P-100s. In the late 1970s General Dynamics proposed a stretched FB-111 with 30,000 lb (13,600 kg) F101-GE-100 engines, as developed for the Rockwell B-1, in place of the standard 20,000 lb (9070 kg) TF30-P-7s. The resulting FB-111H would have had an empty weight of 51,832 lb (23,500 kg), some 64,574 lb (29,285 kg) of internal fuel, and a maximum take-off weight of 140,000 lb (63,490 kg), reaching 155,000 lb (70,295 kg) in flight. Whereas earlier models are capable of Mach 1.1 at sea level and 2.2 at altitude, the FB-111H would have been

Head-on view of a General Dynamics F-111E (66-0022), from the 55th TFS of the 20th TFW, based at RAF Upper Heyford. This photograph emphasises the massive single mainwheels and the sharp wing sweep, which reduces gust response in high-speed penetrations. (Roy Braybrook)

The wing sweep range of the F-111 series is illustrated by this echelon of F-111Cs at an RAAF display in Australia. (John McIver)

A spectacular display is produced by jettisoning fuel between the nozzles of the F-111C and igniting it with afterburner. (John McIver)

limited to Mach 2.0 by simple pitot intakes. Warload-radius performance details for existing F-111s are still classified, but the Pentagon has referred to a HI-LO-LO-HI radius of 600 nm (1100 km) with an 8820 lb (4000 kg) bombload, and a nuclear-strike radius of 800 nm (1480 km) for the FB-111.

America persisted with the F-111 despite its many problems, while Britain quickly abandoned its **TSR.2.** This BAC (Vickers/English Electric) project had its origins in the 1957 OR.339 requirement for a tactical strike/reconnaissance aircraft to replace the Canberra. By 1959 this requirement had been superseded by OR.343, calling for an aircraft to carry an internal load of six 1000 lb (454 kg) bombs over a HI-LO-LO-HI radius of 1000 nm (1850 km). Alternative sorties demanded a 700 nm (1300 km) LO-LO radius at Mach 0.9, and a 550 nm (1020 km) HI-HI radius at Mach 2.0.

The FB-111H was a projected development with more powerful engines and increased internal fuel, offered as a less costly substitute for the Rockwell B-1B. (General Dynamics)

The TSR.2 initially had a maximum design take-off weight of 88,500 lb (40,135 kg) for the required mission performance. However, the RAF wanted to be able to operate from short, badly-surfaced runways, which BAC proposed to do at a reduced weight of 75,000 lb (34,000 kg), giving a radius of 450 nm (835 km). The earlier demand for genuine V/STOL operation was to have been met by the combination of the somewhat lighter English Electric P.17A and a Shorts launch platform equipped with lift engines.

The TSR.2 was powered by two Bristol Siddeley Olympus 22R afterburning turbojets with a design thrust of 30,610 lb (13,880 kg) each. It had automatic terrain following and a Doppler-inertial navigation system to give accuracy at long radius. The programme was cancelled in April 1965 by the new Labour government, on the grounds that development costs had risen well above the original estimates, making it cheaper to buy the F-111.

Instead of the F-111K (as the British version was to be designated) or an Anglo-French variable-geometry (AFVG) aircraft, the RAF eventually received the comparatively small **Panavia Tornado,** which is effectively a compromise between British long-range strike and German close support requirements. Although clearly a poor substitute for TSR.2 in warload-radius terms. The Anglo-Italo-German Tornado was more attractive to British industry in offering the prospect of a long production run (replacing not only Canberras, but also Vulcans, Buccaneers, Jaguars, Lightnings and Phantoms), and in being politically difficult to cancel by virtue of its three-nation status.

The Tornado made its maiden flight on 14 August 1974, and entered service in mid-1982. The basic IDS (interdictor/strike) version has an empty weight of 30,800 lb (14,000 kg), some 11,250 lb (5100 kg) of internal fuel, and a maximum take-off weight of more than 61,500 lb (28,000 kg). It is powered by two afterburning Turbo-Union RB.199 turbofans of around 16,000 lb (7255 kg) thrust. The IDS was followed by the ADV (air defence variant) for Britain, and the ECR (electronic combat and reconnaissance) version is being developed for Germany and Italy.

This second prototype (XR220) of the BAC TSR.2 was completed, but never flew. (BAe)

A Tornado IDS for the Royal
Saudi Air Force, as exhibited at
Farnborough in 1986, with
Hunting JP233 runway attack
weapons under the fuselage. (Roy
Braybrook)

The Luftwaffe Tornado is
intended primarily as a platform
for the MW-1
submunition-dispenser, which was
shown for the first time on
aircraft 43 + 41 at Hanover in
1982. (Roy Braybrook)

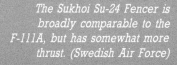

The Sukhoi Su-24 Fencer is broadly comparable to the F-111A, but has somewhat more thrust. (Swedish Air Force)

At time of writing the Tornado production programme amounted to approximately 1000 aircraft. This figure included the original 809 for the air arms of Britain, West Germany, and Italy, some 72 for Saudi Arabia (plus an unspecified number in the second Saudi contract), 8 for Oman (postponed), 35 ECRs for Germany, and 50 attrition aircraft for Britain. In addition, it is anticipated that Italy will have 16 ECR Tornadoes. In late 1988 well over 700 had been delivered, and they had accumulated almost half a million flying hours in service with 25 squadrons in four countries. The IDS brochure gives an interdiction radius of over 550 nm (1020 km) in a LO-LO mission, or over 850 nm (1575 km) in a HI-LO-LO-HI mission, with a typical bombload in each case.

An RAF Tornado in defence-suppression configuration, with seven BAe ALARMs, a pair of fuel tanks, a BOZ-107 chaff/flare dispenser and a Marconi Sky Shadow jammer pod. (BAe)

The third current variable-sweep strike fighter is the Soviet Union's **Sukhoi Su-24 Fencer,** which is broadly comparable in size to the F-111A, but rather better powered, probably to give a high cruise speed without afterburner. The Su-24 is thought to have first flown around 1970, since deliveries reportedly began in late 1974, roughly seven years after the F-111A. By 1986 over 800 were in service. Judging by its size, the Su-24 has an empty weight in the region of 41,000 lb (18,600 kg) and a maximum take-off weight of perhaps 88,000 lb (40,000 kg). It is powered by two afterburning engines which appear to be in the same class as the 25,350 lb (11,500 kg) Tumansky R-29B turbojet of the MiG-27, although a new turbofan may have been developed specifically for this application. According to Pentagon sources, the Su-24 can carry a 6615 lb (3000 kg) warload over a 700 nm (1300 km) mission in a HI-LO-LO-HI profile.

The **Saab-Scania AJ37 Viggen** is somewhat lighter than any of the two seat variable-sweep aircraft discussed above, and it was not designed to deliver nuclear weapons. It nonetheless warrants inclusion in the strike aircraft category, since it can achieve the warload-radius performance specified earlier. The AJ37 may, in fact be regarded as broadly comparable to the F-105 in weight, though the design emphasis was on STOL performance from dispersed sites, rather than high speed penetration with internal warload.

The first of 83 AJ37s for the Swedish Air Force had its maiden flight on 2 February 1967, and the type entered service with F7 wing at Satenas in June 1971. Few weight or performance details have ever been published on the Viggen, but

The Saab-Scania AJ37 Viggen, making its first appearance in splinter camouflage in 1974. This was reportedly the 53rd production aircraft. (Roy Braybrook)

maximum take-off weight is given as 45,200 lb (20,500 kg) with a 7940 lb (3600 kg) external load, and the powerplant for this version is a 26,000 lb (11,800 kg) afterburning Volvo Flygmotor RM8A turbofan. For the proposed export version, which may have had additional pylons, Saab gave a radius with four 1000 lb (454 kg) bombs and external fuel of 460 nm (850 km) LO-LO, and 675 nm (1250 km) HI-LO-HI.

The most interesting technical feature of the Viggen is its STOL performance, which is mainly achieved by virtue of its canard configuration and thrust reversal. At light weight it can take off with a ground roll of only 1300 ft (400 m), and it can land in only 1650 ft (500 m). Landing distance required is minimised by using a mobile precision approach aid to reduce touchdown scatter, and a naval landing technique that eliminates the normal round-out. Down-selection of the undercarriage also lowers the wing-flaps and foreplane-flaps, selects autothrottle to give a constant approach speed, and gives the landing display mode on the HUD. The Viggen's short landing technique demands an extremely strong undercarriage, but with a slow approach, precise touchdown and thrust reversal it allows the aircraft to land on extremely short stretches of highway.

It may be noted that at the preliminary design stage the Swedes considered the use of a variable-sweep wing rather than a fixed canard arrangement, but rejected the swing-wing as a high-risk, high-cost approach to STOL operation.

Two AJ37s of F15 wing of the Swedish Air Force, based at Söderhamn. (A. Anderson, Saab-Scania)

Chapter 5   **Naval Attack Aircraft**

SEVERAL NAVAL AIR ARMS (including those of the Soviet Union and West Germany) employ shore-based aircraft in the anti-shipping strike role, but the term 'naval attack aircraft' is used here in the specific context of types developed to operate from carrier decks.

Deck operation in the traditional form introduces special demands in regard to catapulting and arresting loads, high sink rates on landing, long fatigue life despite these severe once-per-sortie loads, resistance to salt water corrosion, and the need for the nav-attack system to be compatible with flights from a highly mobile deck.

The availability of a catapult may reduce the installed thrust requirement, but landing speed restrictions often demand an extremely high lift coefficient in the approach configuration. In the case of the BAe Buccaneer, some 12 per cent of the engine core flow is bled to provide high-velocity jets over the wing leading edges and the trailing edge flaps, and the tailplane leading edges. For deck operation the associated loss of thrust is acceptable, but in the case of the ground-based export version (operated from hot/high airfields in South Africa) the thrust of the turbine engines has to be augmented by rocket boost. In the case of the Grumman A-6, the jetpipes of the first seven aircraft could be rotated through 23 degrees to provide some jet lift at the expense of the horizontal thrust component, though flight tests proved that the gains did not justify the complexity (due to the A-6's low thrust/weight ratio).

Even in the case of the USN super carriers, the size and weight of the aircraft that can be operated is restricted by catapult and arrester performance, deck strength, and the need to park the greatest possible number of aircraft in the hangar and on the deck. Overall dimensions can be reduced by folding, and it may be noted that the Buccaneer's wingfold has proved useful in RAF operation in terms of facilitating the use of hardened aircraft shelters (HAS). One reason for the popularity of the Douglas A-4 was that its low aspect ratio wing and light weight eliminated the need for a wing-fold.

Span, length and tail height can all be reduced by folding, but there is no way around the weight limit imposed by the carrier design, unless it is argued that V/STOL aircraft in principle avoid the conventional restrictions (due to their independence from carrier equipment and their comparatively gentle touchdown).

Bleeding the engines to provide air for flap-blowing reduces thrust, hence the rocket boost for this Buccaneer S.50, shown undergoing tests with the temporary registration G-2-1. (BAe)

When the RAF adopted the Buccaneer, its wing-fold made it easier to house in shelters. This S.2A (XV360) from No 237 OCU (as indicated by the crosses cutlassed) was photographed at RNAS Yeovilton in 1974. (Roy Braybrook)

The heaviest aircraft to have operated routinely from a carrier is believed to have been the **Douglas A-3B Skywarrior**, which has an empty weight of 39,409 lb (17,875 kg) and in 1959 made a take-off at 84,000 lb (38,100 kg) in KA 3B tanker form. Known to USN deck-crews as 'The Whale', the A-3 has a length of 76.3 ft (23.25 m) and a span of 72.5 ft (22.09 m). It was designed to operate in the heavy attack role, replacing the North American A-2 Savage, which had two piston engines, augmented by an Allison J33 in the rear fuselage for the dash into the target area. The A-2 series (then designated AJ-1) entered service in late 1949, weighed up to 55,000 lb (24,950 kg), and could reach 425 mph (680 km/hr) with three engines turning and burning.

The Douglas A-3 Skywarrior was the US Navy's first all-jet attack aircraft, and probably the world's heaviest carrier-based aircraft. This early example (138915)

The requirement that led to the A-3 specified a 10,000 lb (4535 kg) nuclear weapon and a radius of 1900 nm (3540 km). The Douglas project, with a design gross weight of 68,000 lb (30,830 kg) to suit the *Midway* limit, won, and the XA3D-1 prototype flew on 28 October 1952. Some 283 P&W J57-powered Skywarriors were built, including 164 A-3Bs, and at one stage the type was in service with 18 USN squadrons. During the 1960s many were converted to KA-3B tankers and EA-3B electronic warfare aircraft, the latter having a four-man pressurised cabin in the former bomb-bay. Both variants served with distinction in the Vietnam War, and in a 1987 nose-count the USN was still operating 49 A-3s.

appears to be an A3D-2 (A-3B), with radar bombing system in the nose and a remotely-controlled Westinghouse twin-gun barbette in the tail. (McDonnell Douglas Corp)

The next naval attack aircraft from Douglas was the lightweight A-4 Skyhawk, which flew on 22 June 1954 (and has already been discussed in the ground-based section). The next large USN attack aircraft after the A-3 was the **North American A-5 Vigilante**, which has its maiden flight on 31 August 1958. The A-5 was a response to a 1955 USN requirement, calling for an all-weather Mach 2 replacement for the A-3. The resulting A-5A entered service in mid-1961.

The A-5A had a normal gross weight of 62,000 lb (28,120 kg) and was powered by two afterburning J79-GE-8 turbojets of 17,000 lb (7710 kg) thrust. It cruised at Mach 0.85 and had a Mach 2.0 dash capacity ability. Combat radius was 990 nm (1835 km). The design included a number of advanced features, notably a linear bomb-bay between the engines. The bay held a 2000 lb (910 kg) nuclear weapon, fastened in tandem to two fuel tanks. By the time the target was reached, these tanks were empty and served as a stabilising tail for the weapon, which was ejected backwards out of the bay.

This weapon system was clearly inflexible, and the A-5 was also criticised for its limited range. The A-5B was to have had extra fuel in dorsal and additional external tanks, but was abandoned due to a change in attack policy. From 1962 onwards Vigilantes were removed from the attack role and standardised on the RA-5C reconaissance version, grossing 70,000 lb (31,750 kg).

The British contemporary of the A-5 was the Blackburn (later (BAe) **Buccaneer**, which first flew in S.1 form with de Havilland Gyron Junior turbojet

More representative of later modification standards, this EA-3B (144852/18), from VQ-2 at Rota AB, was photographed at Greenham Common in 1976. (Roy Braybrook)

engines on 30 April 1958. Some 20 development S.1s were built, followed by a production batch of 40 (out of the 50 originally contracted for), which entered service with the RN's 801 Sqn. in 1962 and embarked in HMS *Ark Royal* in February 1963.

For a project that originated in 1955, the Buccaneer has a number of advanced features, including boundary layer control (BLC) for high lift, and Area Rule fuselage shaping to reduce drag and increase rear fuselage equipment space. The internal rotary weapons bay was designed (as in the case of the A-3) primarily to provide the nuclear weapon with a safe environment, a consideration that no longer applies. The Gyron Junior made the Buccaneer underpowered and short of range, hence the Rolls-Royce Spey Mk101 turbofan of 11,030 lb (5000 kg) was introduced as soon as it became available.

Some 84 Buccaneer S.2As were built for the RN, and 64 of these aircraft were later transferred to the RAF, for which service 49 S.2Bs were built. Some S.2As

In the early 1960s the Vigilante was switched from attack to the reconnaissance role, as illustrated by this RA-5C (149276 from RVAH-14 on the USS John F. Kennedy *with ventral sensor pack. (US Navy photograph via Barry Wheeler)*

This montage of photographs by No 809 Sqn of a Royal Navy Buccaneer S.1 (XV865, later converted to an RAF S.2B) shows the rotary bomb-bay in the open position. (HMS Ark Royal)

An RAF Buccaneer armed with four BAe Sea Eagle anti-ship sea-skimming missiles. (BAe)

The ball turret under the nose radome of this Intruder shows it is an A-6E/TRAM, and the 'AC' tail code indicates the carrier is the USS John F. Kennedy. (Grumman Corp)

were later brought to S.2B standard, with provisions for Martel and Sea Eagle missiles and a bulged bomb-bay door allowing an extra 3500 lb (1590 kg) of fuel to be carried in addition to the four 1000 lb (454 kg) internal bombs. The S.2 first flew on 17 May 1963 and entered service two years later. At one stage four squadrons served in *Ark Royal, Eagle, Victorious* and *Hermes*, but from 1975 these last three carriers were withdrawn. In December 1978 the *Ark Royal* was retired and No 809 Sqn, the final RN Buccaneer unit, was disbanded.

In the mid-1960s a batch of 16 Buccaneer S.50s was delivered to the South African Air Force, but a request for a second batch of 16 was turned down by the Foreign Office. The S.50 is used in the maritime strike/reconnaissance role, and differs in having two 250 Imp gal (1135 litre) external tanks and a BS.605 twin-chamber liquid rocket motor in the rear fuselage, giving a take-off boost of 8000 lb (3630 kg) for 30 seconds.

The RAF has used some Buccaneers (Nos 15 and 16 Sqn) in the interdiction/strike role, based at Laarbruch in Germany, but from 1983/84 this wing was re-equipped with the Tornado. The sole remaining RAF Buccaneer wing is now at Lossiemouth in Scotland, where Nos 12 and 208 Sqn will continue in the maritime strike/attack role for several years. Reports suggest that around 70 S.2Bs are available at this base. Few technical details of the Buccaneer have ever been published, but press reports have referred to a maximum take-off weight of about 57,000 lb (25,850 kg). The strong point of the Buccaneer is its high penetration speed of almost 600 knots (1110 km/hr) without afterburner, while carrying four bombs.

The USN equivalent of the Buccaneer is the **Grumman A-6 Intruder**, which came along slightly later and is somewhat slower, but has a more advanced nav-attack system. The requirement was for a day/night all-weather attack aircraft to fill the gap between the lightweight, clear weather A-4 and the heavy A-3 nuclear strike aircraft. The primary mission was the medium attack in a brushfire war, but the aircraft also had to be capable of a nuclear strike in an all-out conflict. The Grumman submission was chosen at the end of 1957.

The maiden flight of the A-6A (then designated A2F-1) took place on 19 April 1960. The design emphasis was on slow approach speeds, so sweep was restricted to 25 degrees at the quarter-chord line, and spoilers were used for lateral control, to leave the wing trailing edge free for flaps. Other unusual features include wingtip-mounted airbrakes. The original airbrakes were mounted immediately behind the jetpipes, to allow a high thrust to be used in the approach and thus ensure a safe overshoot (simply by retracting the airbrakes). The production A-6A was powered by two non-afterburning Pratt & Whitney J52 turbojets of 9300 lb (4220 kg) thrust.

Following operational evaluation by the VX-5 Vampire squadron, aircrew training began with VA-42 'Green Prawns' at NAS Oceana, Virginia, in February 1963. The first operational A-6A unit was VA-75 'Sunday Poachers', which deployed on board the CVA-62 *Independence* in May 1965, sailing from Norfolk, Virginia. The carrier was assigned to the US 7th Fleet operating off Vietnam, and VA-75 carried out its first operational sorties with the A-6A on 1 July 1965. Some three months were spent on 'Yankee Station' in the Gulf of Tonkin, carrying out attacks on North Vietnamese factories, airfields, ports, SAM sites, ammunition and

An A-6E in defence-suppression configuration, with 10 Mk 82 bombs and two AGM-88A HARMs. (Grumman Corp)

fuel dumps, and road and rail bridges. The carrier later operated on the 'Dixie Station' off South Vietnam, with the VA-75 attacking Vietcong concentrations and acting as pathfinders for A-4s and F-4s.

The A-6As operated by the USN took part in a series of carrier-based deployments, but USMC aircraft were also operated from Vietnamese airfields, notably Da Nang. The first deployment was made by VMA-242 'Batman' from MCAS El Toro, California, the first such operational missions being flown in November 1966. A typical armament was 28 Mk 82 500 lb (227 kg) or five Mk 84 2000 lb (910 kg) bombs.

The A-6A proved its ability to operate in all weathers and to carry out blind bombing attacks against sore-thumb radar targets such as bridges and power stations. On the other hand the nav-attack system required a massive maintenance effort, and three out of the four aircrafts lost on the first deployment were destroyed by their own bombs colliding and exploding just after release in dive attacks.

A total of 488 A-6As were built, some of which were later converted to A-6B defence suppression aircraft, A-6Cs with FLIR and LLTV, and KA-6D tankers. The definitive attack variant (at time of writing) is the A-6E/TRAM (Target Recognition and Attack, Multisensor), to which standard remaining A-6As are being updated. The A-6E introduced a revised nav-attack system, including a Norden APQ-148 radar with simultaneous terrain clearance, ground mapping and target tracking facilities. This model first flew on 27 February 1970, with deliveries following in September 1971. The TRAM system came later, adding a ball turret under the front fuselage, housing a Hughes FLIR and laser ranger/designator. The current aircraft also has the Litton CAINS (Carrier Airborne Inertial Navigation System) and the Sperry ACLS (Automatic Carrier Landing System).

The fully-equipped A-6E/TRAM was deployed with the VA-165 'Boomers' in the CVA-64 *Constellation* in 1977. All A-6Es are being modified to take the AGM-84A Harpoon anti-ship missile, and the USN plans a total of 12 A-6E and four KA-6D squadrons, in addition to the five USMC A-6E squadrons.

The A-6E is powered by two 9300 lb (4220 kg) J52-P-8Bs, and has an empty weight of 26,745 lb (12,130 kg). Internal fuel is 15,940 lb (7230 kg). Maximum take-off weight is 58,600 lb (26,580 kg) in the case of a catapult launch, though a marginally higher weight can be flown from an airfield. Maximum speed at sea level is 560 knots (1040 km/hr).

An A-6E (160996) of VA-35, assigned to carrier air wing CVW-8 embarked aboard the USS Nimitz, about to touch down. (US Navy photograph, via Robert F Dorr).

In 1984 the USN began funding development of what was initially termed an A-6E Upgrade, and later the A-6F Intruder II. Modifications included the introduction of 10,800 lb (4900 kg) F404-GE-400D turbofans, the new Norden APQ-173 radar, a passive night-attack system, air-to-air weapons in the form of AIM-9s or -120s (AMRAAMs) on two additional wing pylons, a considerable revised cockpit, and new avionics that included Collins GPS. The first of five development A-6Fs had its maiden flight on 25 August 1987, and the procurement of 150 was planned by 1995. However, in the course of getting the FY89 defence budget through Congress the A-6F programme was deleted, as was procurement of the A-6E beyond FY88. Grumman is nonetheless hoping to keep work on the A-6 going with a proposal to upgrade 167 A-6Es to A-6Gs, with some of the A-6F improvements. The EA-6B Prowler is an unarmed electronics warfare derivative of the Intruder. It first flew on 25 May 1968 and saw service with two USN squadrons over SE Asia in late 1972.

The use of the **Vought A-7 Corsair II** by the USAF has already been discussed in the ground attack section. The US Navy's A-7A first flew on 27 September 1965, and deliveries began in the following year. Operational sorties were flown over Vietnam by the first A-7A unit, VA-147 'Jasons', flying from the USS *Ranger* (CVA-61) in late 1967. The A-7A had a non-afterburning 11,350 lb (5150 kg) TF30-P-6 turbofan, and it was joined in USN service by the A-7B with the 12,000 lb (5440 kg) TF30-P-8. Some 199 A-7As and 196 A-7Bs were built. The A-7B was later equipped with the TF30-P-408 of 13,400 lb (6080 kg) thrust, this engine also being used in the A-7C, of which 67 were built.

The US Navy's old-fashioned high-visibility markings are exemplified by this A-7E (159294) from VA-83 'Rampagers' exhibited at Le Bourget in 1975, the 'AA' tail-code then signifying CVW-17 from the USS Forrestal. (Roy Braybrook)

The A-7 was intentionally a low-risk project, derived loosely from the supersonic F-8 Crusader. The basic airframe-engine combination thus incorporated few features of technical interest, but the A-7 did have an advanced nav-attack system, with Doppler-inertial navigation and a central digital computer. In the knowledge that A-7s would be involved in a real shooting war, the type accumulated 430 lb (195 kg) of armour to protect the pilot, engine and fuel lines.

The only development problem of note was that the A-7A encountered difficulties due to steam ingestion from the catapult, reducing take-off weight from 41,500 to 38,000 lb (18,800 to 17,250 kg). This problem was solved by opening a 12th-stage bleed on the TF30, and by applying a better sealant to the catapult.

Following USAF-funded development of the A-7D with the Allison TF41 Spey and M61 Gatling gun, the USN adopted the basically similar A-7E, but with an uprated 15,000 lb (6800 kg) TF41-A-2. The A-7E first flew on 25 November 1968, and the first of 505 production aircraft was delivered in July 1969.

An A-7B (154375) from VA-72 'Black Hawks' on show at Greenham Common in 1977. The 'AB' tail-code of CVW-1 from the USS John F. Kennedy *is repeated on the F-14A of VF-14 'Top Hatters' in the background. (Roy Braybrook)*

Ironically, the Navy's A-7E, flying with VA-146 'Blue Diamonds' and VA-147 'Jasons' from the USS *America* (CV-66), entered service off the Vietnamese coast in May 1970, more than two years ahead of the A-7D from which it was derived. In all, 27 Navy A-7 squadrons took part in that war, some 395 A-7A/Bs flying 49,200 combat missions, and 387 A-7Es flying 41,030. Only 54 Navy A-7s were lost to enemy fire, an average rate of 0.06 per cent.

The A-7E has an empty weight of 19.048 lb (8640 kg) and carries 10,173 lb (4615 kg) of fuel internally. Maximum catapult take-off weight is 42,000 lb (19,050 kg). Carrying a dozen Mk 82 bombs, the A-7E can reach 545 knots (1010 km/hr) at low level. With 60 per cent fuel, two AIM-9s and 1000 rounds of 20 mm ammunition, the A-7E has a sustained turn performance of 5G at sea level. Taking off at 37,540 lb (17,025 kg) with 12 Mk 82 bombs on two pylons, the A-7E has a HI-LO-HI radius of almost 600 nm (1110 km).

A Sea Harrier of No 800 Sqn in post-Falklands dark sea grey, positioned on the deck of HMS Hermes *(R12), which was the flag-ship of the 1982 Task Force. (Philip Boyden, BAe)*

Although the most significant operational use of the A-7 series occurred during the Vietnam War, it should also be noted that A-7Es were employed in Operation Prairie Fire against Libya in March 1986, firing AGM-88 HARMs against the SA-5 launch site at Sirte. Meanwhile, the A-6Es used Harpoons and Rockeye CBUs against Libyan patrol boats. In the following month 12 A-6Es participating in Operation El Dorado Canyon attacked two targets near Banghazi, using their Norden APQ-148 radars and Hughes AAS-33 FLIRs, while other A-6Es joined F/A-18s in firing 30 HARMs and 12 Shrikes against Libyan air defence radars.

Britain's principal contribution to naval attack development has been the **BAe Sea Harrier** V/STOL aircraft, although it is primarily an air defence fighter with a secondary reconnaissance role. Anti-shipping strike sorties with Sea Eagle guided weapons or nuclear bombs is third in order of importance.

A navalised, radar-equipped derivative of the RAF's Harrier GR3, which first flew on 31 August 1966 and entered service in 1969, the Sea Harrier had its maiden flight on 20 August 1978. Both variants are powered by the 21,500 lb (9750 kg) Rolls-Royce Pegasus vectored-thrust turbofan, and both have 5060 lb (2295 kg) of internal fuel, but the Sea Harrier has a somewhat heavier empty weight at 14,052 lb (6373 kg) and a higher gross weight, currently given as 26,200 lb (11,880 kg), compared to the 25,200 lb (11,430 kg) of the GR3. Both models are capable of 635 knots (1177 km/hr) clean at sea level. The Sea Harrier has a HI-LO-HI radius of 200 nm (370 km) with two Sea Eagle anti-ship missiles and two 30 mm cannon.

Considering that the Harrier GR3 and Sea Harrier were the first practical high performance V/STOL aircraft, the production run has been disappointing. The RAF bought 124 Harrier GR1/3s and 27 two seaters, the USMC102 AV-8As and 8 two-seaters, and the Spanish Navy 11 AV-8ASs and 2 two-seaters, while the RN bought 57 Sea Harriers and 4 two-seaters, and the Indian Navy 23 Sea Harriers and 4 two-seaters.

Both the Sea Harrier and the GR3 were used in the Falklands conflict of 1982, In total, some 28 Sea Harriers and 14 GR3s were involved, operating from the carriers *Hermes* and *Invincible* under the control of the Fleet Air Arm's Nos 800 and 801 Sqn and the RAF's No 1 (F) Sqn. The air war was very short, lasting only from May 1st to June 14th, but these first generation Harriers did demonstrate a remarkable flexibility, operating from the carriers and a variety of VTOL pads on container ships, support vessels, and from forward airstrips.

The role played by Argentine Navy **Dassault Breguet Super Etendards** was confined to Exocet attacks. At the outbreak of hostilities five aircraft (out of 14 ordered) and five missiles had been delivered, and one aircraft was grounded to provide spares. The remaining four flew five missions (10 sorties), in the course of which all five Exocets were fired. Three appear to have missed their targets, but the Type 42 destroyer *Sheffield* and the container ship *Atlantic Conveyor* were destroyed.

To digress, the Exocet was to be further tested in the so-called 'tanker war' in the Persian Gulf, in which most of the kills were attributed to Exocets launched

Artist's impression of the Sea Harrier updated to FRS.2 standard with Ferranti Blue Vixen pulse-Doppler radar and AIM-120 beyond-visual-range AAMs. (BAe)

from Iraqi Mirage F1EQs. Iraq's 'turkey shoot' went badly wrong on 17 May 1987, when two Exocets were launched against a radar target that turned out to be the 3585-ton USN frigate *Stark*. Both missiles hit, though one failed to explode. Of the 221 officers and men aboard, 37 died, and the ship was extensively damaged.

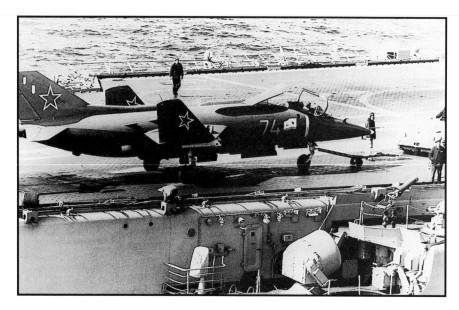

The Yak-38 Forger VTOL aircraft is believed to have a limited attack capability, though it lacks the operational flexibility of the Sea Harrier. (US Navy photograph, via Robert F. Dorr).

Opposite: *The first of 70 super Etendard of France's Aéronavale being positioned for a catapult launch. (Dassault-Breguet)*

The Super Etendard engages an arrester wire. (Dassault-Breguet)

Returning to the subject of the Super Etendard, this aircraft first flew on 24 November 1977, and 71 examples have been purchased by the French Navy, with deliveries running from mid-1978. It is powered by a non-afterburning SNECMA Atar 8K-50 turbojet of 11,000 lb (5000 kg) thrust, and has an empty weight of 14,320 lb (6500 kg). Normal mission weight is 20,800 lb (9450 kg), but the Super Etendard may be launched at up to 26,400 lb (11,900 kg). The aircraft is capable of 650 knots (1200 km/hr) at sea level, and has a radius of 474 nm (880 km) in the anti-ship mission. Around 50 French Navy Super Etendards are being updated, the modifications including provisions for the Aerospatiale ASMP nuclear weapon.

Looking to the future, the only significant naval attack aircraft project is the USN's A-12 (formerly ATA or Advanced Tactical Aircraft). Very little has been published of this programme, beyond the fact that the A-12 will replace the A-6 series, and that survivability is emphasised, implying stealth technology. In December 1987 the General Dynamics/McDonnell Douglas team was selected for the full-scale engineering development (FSED) phase, which expected to lead to first flight around 1992 and service entry in the mid 1990s. The engine will probably be improved General Electric F404 turbofans. The USN is expected to buy around 450 A-12s, and the USAF is to consider this aircraft as a possible replacement for the F-111 and F-15E.

Chapter 6   **Attack Helicopters**

FOR PRACTICAL PURPOSES the helicopter appeared just before the end of WWII. Due to the heavy weight of piston engines, disposable load was extremely limited, and rotary-wing aircraft were consequently restricted to light liaison duties and short-range rescue missions. The level of technology had barely changed by the time of the Korean War, when Bell Model 47s airlifted around 25,000 casualties back to MASH units, making a significant difference to a soldier's chance of surviving front-line wounds.

The French were the first to apply lightweight turbine engines to helicopters, and these powerplants (though more expensive and thirstier than piston engines) made possible much higher loads. France had also pioneered the development of wire-guided anti-tank guided weapons (ATGWs). It was thus a natural move for the French Army in Algeria to arm the (turbine-engined) Alouette II with SS.10 and 11 missiles and use them to attack insurgents' vehicles, bunkers and weapon emplacements. Other armament fits included machine guns and small rocket pods on Army Vertol H-21s and 20 mm cannon on Air Force H-34s (S-58s). The concept of an attack helicopter had been combat-proven in this 1954–62 conflict, though the Alouette was far removed from the idea of a dedicated weapons platform, as were the H-21 and H-34.

The US Army and Marine Corps had long been interested in having an armed helicopter, though they had been thwarted by shortcomings in powerplant and armament technology. The first recorded trials had taken place in 1942, when the US Army fitted a 20 mm cannon to a Sikorsky R4. Further experiments were carried out in the 1950s, including USMC firings of the SS.11 and (in 1960) Bullpup missiles, but it was the outbreak of the Vietnam War in 1965 that forced the pace of development. In essence, the US services tried to win where the French Army had failed, by using the superior mobility provided by rotary-wing aircraft. However, if utility helicopters were to inject eight-man sections of troops into hostile areas, they needed supporting firepower that could be continued right into the landing zone (LZ). This was done initially by replacing some or all of the troops in the cabin with weapons. Since it was undesirable to land half a section, the preferred solution was the dedicated gunship, which could be faster and would present a smaller target if designed solely for that role.

The principal helicopter of the Vietnam War was the **Bell UH-1 'Huey'**, of which that company was building up to 150 per month (aside from the 'Cobra'

The French pioneered the use of attack helicopters in Algeria in 1954-62. This Alouette is armed with SS.11 missiles. (Aérospatiale)

gunships) in the late 1960s. Over 10,000 Hueys have seen military service. The first Bell Model 204 had its maiden flight on 22 October 1956, and it was ordered into production as the HU-1A Iroquois, this initial designation giving rise to the nickname 'Huey'. The type served in Vietnam from April 1962, when five HU-1As of the US Army's 57th Medical Detachment arrived to complement the CH-21C Shawnees of the 8th and 57th Transportation Companies, which had arrived in the previous December to give ARVN troops an air assault capability. During the subsequent peak years of 1967–70 Hueys made up over 50 per cent of the US Army helicopter force in SE Asia, a force that reached 3926 aircraft in March 1970.

Although the Vietcong were initially badly armed, it was soon discovered that airmobile operations with the CH-21C 'Flying Banana' were hazardous, due to inadequate supporting fire. Artillery and mortar fire had to be directed more than 1000 metres from the LZ due to their inaccuracy, and VNAF attacks with napalm and bombs often created dangerous conditions for the landing. Efforts were therefore made to mount light machine guns in the helicopter doorways (often by suspending the guns by elastic cords attached to the roof). but these were of limited effectiveness.

In the course of 1962 some heavier armaments were tested on the UH-1As (the new designation came into use from 18 September 1962) of the US Army's first armed helicopter company. This was the Utility Tactical Transport Helicopter Company (UTTHCO), which was formed on July 25th in Okinawa, and reached

Vietnam via Thailand on October 9th. The armaments used included skid-mounted 7.62 mm M-37C and M-60C machine guns and seven/eight-tube 2.75-inch (70 mm) FFAR pods. These forward-firing (fixed) weapons were installed in addition to the pair of flexibly-mounted lateral 7.62 mm M-60D machine guns, which each had a 500-round ammunition box attached to the base tube assembly, and was designated as the M-23 Armament Subsystem.

The concept of a Huey gunship took a further step forward on 20 November 1962 with the arrival at Tan Son Nhut airport of the first UH-1Bs, in which the 700 shp T53-L-1 engine of the UH-1A was replaced by the 825 shp L-5. This first dedicated attack variant (like the USMC's UH-1E) also had what became known as the M-6 Armament Subsystem, developed by Emerson Electric. The M-6 had provisions for four M-60Cs discharging a total of 4400 rd/min over an effective range of up to 2250 ft (685 m), or XM-3 rocket launchers of SS-11 ATGWs. The four guns were controlled in azimuth and elevation by the copilot, using a roof-mounted sight, and had a total of 6700 rounds available in 12 floor-mounted boxes and the flexible feed-chutes. These forward hemisphere weapons were augmented by two bungee-mounted M-60s fired by the door gunners.

Between mid-October 1962 and mid-March 1963 the armed helicopter concept was formally evaluated by the US Army in Vietnam, using the UH-1B to assess the practicality of using the Huey to escort transport helicopters and for fire suppression around the LZ. Armed Hueys proved valuable in both roles, but the high drag of the gunship made it 20 knots (37 km/hr) slower than the troop-carrying 'slick', hence air assault operations were slowed by the escorts.

A further problem was the increasing effectiveness of Vietcong return fire. At

These RAAF Hueys were photographed at Fairbairn (Canberra) in 1976. The example in the foreground (A2-720) is a UH-1B, formerly US Army 63-9790, and in the background is a UH-1H (A2-310). During the Vietnam War a number of UH-1Bs and -1Ds of No 9 Sqn, which formed part of the First Australian Task Force, were converted to gunships. The standard armament was two 7.62 mm Miniguns, two seven-tube RP launchers, and two door-mounted 7.62 mm M60 machine guns. (Roy Braybrook)

the Battle of Ap Bac in early 1963 the insurgents introduced 12.7 and 14.5 mm heavy machine guns that outranged the 7.62 mm of the UH-1B by a large margin. Four out of the ten CH-21s used in the assault were shot down, as was one of the five escorting UH-1Bs.

The speed deficiency of the UH-1B was to some degree overcome by the introduction into service of the UH-1C in 1966, with the uprated T53-L-9, increased chord blades, a new rotor hub, and a 1000lb (454 kg) increase in disposable load.

However, in 1964 the US Army had established a need for a helicopter designed from the outset for the attack role, and in March 1966 the Lockheed AH-56A Cheyenne was selected for development. Although potentially a highly effective attack helicopter, the AH-56A was too complex for quick development, and the programme was eventually abandoned after the prototype crashed at Farnborough in 1974.

The US Army's XM-3 Armament Subsystem appears to have been similar to this 81 mm SNORA installation, but with 24 individual tubes on each side instead of 21. (Oerlikon)

The Lockheed AH-56A Cheyenne was abandoned in the mid-1970s, but it paved the way for the AH-64, which had its maiden flight on 30 September 1975. (Lockheed-California Co)

In the meantime Bell had built a private-venture attack derivative of the UH-1 series, the Model 209, which followed an earlier tandem-seat project named the Sioux Scout. The Bell 209 first flew on 7 September 1965, and the concept was in due course adopted by the US Army as the basis for its interim attack helicopter, the AH-1 HueyCobra.

Development of the HueyCobra was comparatively straightforward, but it was not until 1967 that the first production series (AH-1G) entered service, hence the UH-1B/C were left to perform the armed helicopter tasks for some of the most difficult years of the war.

This continuing responsibility led to a series of armament developments. Combining the four-gun M-6 system with two seven-round rocket pods, which were fired by the pilot and had an effective range of more than 8000 ft (2500 m), produced the M-16 system. Replacing the four M-60C machine guns of the M-6 with two M-134 7.62 mm General Electric Miniguns produced the M-21. Each Minigun fired at 2000 rd/min, and was therefore fitted with a 3-second burst-limiter, although the Huey carried a total of 6400 rounds for these weapons.

The name 'Hog' was applied to a Huey with an XM-3 system, consisting of two 24-tube batteries of M-151 rockets, while the 'Heavy Hog' combined the XM-3 with a 40 mm M-5 grenade-launcher in an M-75 chin turret, equipped with 150 (and later 302) rounds. The M-5 had a cyclic rate of 220 rd/min and an effective range of 4900 ft (1500 m).

The rocket projectile (RP) gave the Huey the means to out-range a heavy machine gun on the ground, without the high recoil loads of a cannon. Once RPs had been cleared for use from the helicopter, it was a natural development to extend its use from the escort and fire support roles to attacking targets beyond the immediate zone of ground combat. The result was the formation of two battalions of ARA or Aerial Rocket Artillery: the 2nd Battn, 20th ARA, which formed part of the 1st Cavalry Division (Airmobile), and the 4th Bttn, 77th ARA, forming part of the 101st Airborne Division (Airmobile).

The basic operational unit was a section of two UH-1B/Cs, generally equipped with XM-3 rocket systems, later superseded by AH-1Gs, each with up to four XM-159 19-tube FFAR batteries. Two sections formed a platoon, three platoons formed a battery, and three batteries (together with the command and control section of three UH-1B/Cs) made up the battalion. Each battery held at least one section on constant alert. In a typical mission, ARA helicopters were off the ground within 2.5 min, had a transit time of 11 min, and were placing rockets on the target (having fired several for aiming point correction) within 24 minutes of the call for support having been received.

It is clear that, of the US services, the Army led in the development of the attack helicopter, since the Marine Corps relied mainly on its (fixed-wing) A-4s for air support. Nonetheless, in April 1963 USMC UH-34D Sea Horses taking part in an assault operation had to be escorted by a detachment of Army UH-1Bs, and this soon became regular practice. The result was the development of the UH-1E specifically to suit Marine needs, with a brake to stop the rotor quickly after a deck landing, and magnesium parts replaced by aluminium to reduce salt water corrosion. The UH-1E was typically armed with the TK-2 (Temporary Kit 2) system, combining four side-mounted M-60C machine guns (fixed to fire straight ahead) and two FFAR rocket pods, later supplemented by two more M-60s in an Emerson Electric TAT-101 chin turret. From 1969 the UH-1Es began to be replaced by AH-1Gs.

Returning to the subject of Army UH-1B/C armament developments, provisions were made on some of these aircraft to take up to six AGM-22B (French SS.11) ATGWs, with what was designated the M22 system. The missiles weighed 64 lb (29 kg) each, and had a firing range of up to 11,500 ft (3500 m). They were launched and guided by the co-pilot, using a small control stick. The M-22 system was first used operationally in October 1965 by the 2/20th ARA against Vietcong bunkers. Since there was little call during that stage of the war for precision attacks against hard targets, a more flexible arrangement (the Maxwell System) was developed, in which provisions for two AGM-22Bs were added to a pair of XM-3 rocket pods. The M-22 system was not used in the anti-tank role until the final phase of the war, when UH-1Ms killed a T-54A tank and a PT-76 amphibious light tank in May 1972, with the expenditure of nine and six missiles respectively. A further five were used against another PT-76, but this was only damaged.

Before expanding on anti-tank operations in Vietnam, it is relevant to outline the development of the **AH-1G HueyCobra**, which played a major role in these actions. The AH-1 has a significant degree of commonality with the utility series, but a slender 38 inch (96.5 cm) fuselage to reduce drag and projected target area. The dynamic system was based on that of the UH-1C, with its wide-chord blades, but the Bell-patented stabiliser bar was replaced by a SCAS (stability and control augmentation system). The two crew members were seated in tandem, with the gunner in front for the best possible field of view.

A US Army AH-1G HueyCobra (believed to be 67-15800) on show at RAF Woodbridge in 1976, armed with RP pods and a twin M-129 40 mm grenade-launcher in the chin turret. (Roy Braybrook)

The fixed (ie, permanent) armament of the AH-1 is mounted in a chin turret. Initial production AH-1Gs had a TAT-102A housing a 7.62 mm General Electric M-134 Minigun supplied with 8000 rounds. This was superseded by the XM-28A1 with two Miniguns or two 40 mm M-129 grenade launchers, or a Minigun and an M-129 in combination. External loads are mounted on four hardpoints on stub-wings, typical stores used in Vietnam being XM-157/-158/-159 rocket pods, the XM-18 Minigun pod, and the 20 mm XM-159 cannon pod. The 20 mm cannon provided the capability to outrange the Vietcong's heavy machine guns, but this gun was initially available only in the form of the six-barrel M61 Vulcan gun, which was technically capable of firing up to 7200 rd/min. When the gun was derated to 750 rd/min to suit helicopter applications, it was clearly unnecessarily heavy for the fire support task. The same job could be done with only three barrels, and thus the M197 was born.

In addition to combining an unprecedented armament with a maximum level speed of 140 knots (260 km/hr), the AH-1G brought a new survivability to rotary-wing attack operations. It had 223 lb (101 kg) of armour for the crew, the engine, and other vital components. It had self-sealing fuel tanks and (following the introduction of the SA-7 in the first half of 1972) a 'toilet bowl' IR-suppression device for the exhaust, and flare dispensers.

The first AH-1Gs arrived in Vietnam in August 1967, and the first operational mission was flown on September 4th, although the type was still officially under test. The first AH-1G combat unit was the 1st Platoon of the Army's 334th Armed Helicopter Company, which previously operated UH-1Cs, and flew its first Cobra missions on October 8th.

Attack helicopters were able to provide much closer support for friendly forces than was possible with fixed-wing bombing runs. In daylight direct fire support missions, the normal safety margins were 150 ft (45 m) for machine guns, 180 ft (55 m) for grenades, and 210 ft (65 m) for RPs, compared to 750 ft (230 m) for the smallest bomb in use. In emergency these figures could be reduced by around 50 per cent (or more, at the discretion of the commander on the ground), but at night they were increased by two-thirds.

Even before the arrival of the Cobras, efforts had been made to continue armed helicopter operations into the hours of darkness. The 'Lighting Bug' programme of 1965 (later redesignated 'Firefly') employed one UH-1B fitted with seven C-123 landing lights to provide surface illumination for a pair of gunships, mainly in operations against Vietcong sampans in the south of the country. This array of lights was later replaced by a single, more powerful (20 kW) searchlight, allowing the illuminator to cruise higher. A further refinement was the 'Nighthawk' system, in which one Huey used a combination of IR searchlight and a 'starlight scope' to detect targets, then illuminated them with white light for the gunships. Some UH-1Ms were equipped with Hughes Aircraft ASQ-132 LLTV sensors and others with AAQ-5 FLIR, both used in combination with the M-21 armament system.

Some Cobras were equipped with LLTV under the CONFICS (CObra Night FIre Control System) programme, and later with the combination of AAQ-5 FLIR and APQ-137 MTI radar, the system being known as SMASH (Southeast Asia Multi-Sensor Armament Subsystem for HueyCobra).

In 1969 President Nixon had begun to withdraw US forces in line with his declared aim of 'Vietnamizing' what appeared to be a diminishing conflict. By the end of March 1972 American military manpower in Vietnam was down from 500,000 to 95,000, and the VNAF was flying three-quarters of the in-country operational sorties.

On 30 March 1972 the NVA struck south across the Demilitarized Zone (DMZ) with three divisions numbering 40,000 men, supported by T-54, T-34 and PT-76 tanks, 130 mm artillery with a range of 17 miles (27 km), and SA-2 and SA-7 missiles. While this main force invaded Military Region I (MR-I), other major drives were made from Cambodia into MR-II and MR-III. In MR-I at least the air defence environment was far worse than anything previously encountered in South Vietnam: in addition to 23 and 37 mm, the NVA had brought in radar-predicted 57, 85 and 100 mm guns.

The response of all the US services in redeploying units to SE Asia was remarkable by any standards. In addition, in only four days 1000 FFARs with the new XM-247 dual-purpose (anti-tank, anti-personnel) warhead had been manufactured, and they reached Vietnam on April 15th. Prior to this date armed helicopters had been restricted to HE, white phosphorus and an old Mk V HEAT warhead. The FFARs appear to have been delivered in comparatively steep (30-35 degree) dive attacks, partly to attack the thinner armour on the top of the tank, and partly because (unlike the UH-1) the AH-1G was somewhat vulnerable to fire from the sides. Despite the limitations of the FFAR, by May 11th AH-1Gs had destroyed 10 T-54s and 3 PT-76s, and had damaged a further 6 T-54s.

However, the key anti-tank weapon of this 1972 Easter Offensive was the Hughes Aircraft TOW missile, which had been deployed to Vietnam in 1970 in ground-mounted form, but had not been used operationally. In airborne form TOW was developed as the XM-26 system (complete with stabilised sight) for the ill-fated Cheyenne helicopter. When South Vietnam was invaded, two UH-1Bs that had been used earlier in the SM-26 trials were found at Fort Lewis, Washington, re-equipped with the XM-26 and flown to the war zone by C-141. The UH-1Bs and a batch of TOWs arrived at Tan Son Nhut on April 24th, and Army aviators were given a short course on the XM-26, graduating after the firing of two rounds.

On April 28th the two TOW-capable Hueys (redesignated NUH-1Bs) were repositioned to Camp Holloway near Pleiku, and on May 2nd the first operational firings took place, destroying four captured US M-41 tanks and one truck near Kontum. Although Raytheon Hawk SAMs had been used successfully by the Israelis in 1967, and US soldiers had fired French missiles earlier in the Vietnam war, this was the first time that American GW had been fired by US soldiers in combat.

In the main attack on Kontum on May 26th, the two NUH-1Bs fired 21 TOWs, killing 9 tanks. In the course of May and June the temporary duty (TDY) team fired a total of 94 TOWs in combat, resulting in 81 hits and the destruction of 24 tanks, 4 APCs and numerous other targets. The two Hueys were then handed over to the 1st Aviation Brigade, and remained in Vietnam until late January 1973. Aside from 37 rounds fired in training, some 162 were fired in combat, of which 124 (ie, 77 per cent) scored direct hits. The targets killed included 27 tanks, 21 trucks, 5 APCs and 8 bunkers. There were 11 cases of guidance failure, and in 4 instances the missile guided but had been fired outside the 9840 ft (3000 m) limit of the guidance wires. Notwithstanding this very small percentage of failures, this new helicopter-launched ATGW had proved itself an outstanding success in its first operational deployment.

There was no intention to make TOW a standard fit for the UH-1, but the XM-26 armament system was applied (following cancellation of the Cheyenne) as an upgrade for the AH-1G, and tests with the production Cobra-TOW combination began in June 1975. On a similar timescale deliveries also began of Cobras with the improved M-65 armament system in place of the XM-26.

South Atlantic 1982

The Falklands/Malvinas conflict between Britain and Argentina involved some use of ground-based armed helicopters, but it was more notable for the first operational employment of anti-ship GW.

On the Argentine side the type closest to a gunship was the Agusta A.109A, of which the *Ejercito* (Army) deployed three to the islands. The A.109A was armed with forward-firing machine gun and rocket pods, but these weapons were reportedly not used operationally. Nine UH-1Hs and five Pumas were also deployed and were fitted with flexibly-mounted side guns, but were mainly used to move troops to remote outposts.

On the British side the Royal Marines sent six Scout AH.1s and nine Gazelle AH.1s of the 3rd Commando Brigade Air Sqn, while the Army sent six Scouts and six Gazelles from the Army Air Corps' No 656 Sqn. A total of 16 Gazelles were modified to war standard at Middle Wallop, the changes including provisions for two six-round Matra pods of 68 mm SNEB rockets, which were needed primarily to put down smoke. At Ascension the Marines' Gazelles were fitted with flexibly-mounted 7.62 mm GPMGs in the left doorway, using spare mounts from Volvo BV.202 snow vehicles.

In the event the lack of natural cover on the islands largely restricted the use of these helicopters to reconnaissance, though both types were used to escort the RAF's sole surviving Chinook. The stabilised magnifying sight fitted to the Scout was useful both in reconnaissance and in firing SS.11 missiles against point targets, but the Gazelle (with no such sight) was mainly relegated to casualty evacuation and emergency supply duties.

Naval helicopters had seen action long before the amphibious landing at San Carlos. During the preceding Operation Paraquat to liberate South Georgia, the County-class destroyer *Antrim* had detected an Argentine submarine, the 1870-ton *Santa Fé*, late on April 24th. On the morning of the 25th the *Antrim's* Wessex HAS.3 (from No 737 Sqn) found the submarine, which had been landing troops at Grytviken. Two depth charges from the Wessex forced it to surface, then a pair of Wasps HAS.1s of No 829 Sqn were called up from the Rothsay-class frigate *Plymouth* and the ice patrol ship *Endurance*. The Wasps obtained hits on the conning tower with AS.12 missiles, and the *Santa Fé* limped back to Grytviken, before being towed to the old whaling station, where it sank alongside the jetty.

Following the arrival of the Carrier Battle Group in the area of the Falklands, Sea Kings began radar surface searches, and early in the morning of May 3rd one of these helicopters was fired on by an ocean-going patrol boat, the *Alferez*

Sobral. Two **Lynx HAS.2s** of No 815 Sqn were called up from the Type 42 guided missile destroyers *Coventry* and *Glasgow,* and engaged the boat with the BAe Sea Skua missile, which was technically still in the middle of acceptance trials. Two days later their target limped into Puerto Deseado, her bridge blown away and the captain and seven members of the crew dead.

This Royal Marines Gazelle AH.1 (XX412) of the 3rd Commando Brigade Air Sqn was exhibited at Middle Wallop shortly after the Falklands conflict. It had a 7.62 mm GPMG mounted in the left doorway and a rack carrying a six-tube 68 mm RP pod and flare attachments on each side. (Roy Braybrook)

On May 23rd the Lynx from the Type 21 frigate *Antelope* was tasked with attacking the Argentine supply vessel *Rio Carcarana,* which had previously been attacked by Sea Harriers. Both Sea Skuas scored direct hits, and the ship caught fire and sank.

The final Sea Skua firing occurred on June 13th, when the Lynx from the Leander-class frigate *Penelope* attacked the patrol craft *Rio Iguazu.* which had previously been strafed by Sea Harriers and beached. On this occasion the missile appears to have struck high, causing only minor damage to the bridge.

More than 400 AH-1Gs were modified to the Modernized AH-1S configuration, like this example with three-barrel M197 20 mm turret and TOW launchers. In addition, over 130 new-build AH-1Ss have been manufactured.
(Bell Helicopter Textron)

This Argentine Army A.109A (AE-331) was captured by the Royal Marines at Port Stanley race course on 14 June 1982, armed with 7.62 mm machine gun pods and seven-tube RP clusters. It was brought back to the UK and given the British serial ZE411. (Roy Braybrook)

Current Developments

The experience of the Vietnam War gave the US a head-start in the development of the dedicated attack helicopter (at least in the land-based context), and the resulting Cobra-TOW combination was adopted by several other countries, including Iran, Israel and Japan. The Spanish Navy purchased 8 AH-1Gs for anti-ship strikes, but the Cobra has not been widely adopted in Europe. Aside from the fact that European manufacturers can develop perfectly satisfactory helicopters, there may also have been objections that early Cobras were not equipped for European conditions, and also that a two-man gunship lacks operational flexibility. Over the last 10–15 years such views have been modified, and at time of writing there appears to be a good chance that later US attack helicopters (eg, advanced versions of the AH-64) may be accepted by some European services.

The British Army introduced the multi-role **Westland Lynx** at the end of the 1970s, and in March 1981 the TOW-version reached operational status with No 654 Sqn of 4 Regiment, Army Air Corps (AAC) at Detmold in Germany. The Lynx might be regarded as a twin-engined British equivalent of the Huey, which can place and relocate sections of troops with man-portable ATGW, in addition to making direct attacks on tanks. The basic AH.1 has two R-R Gem 2 engines of 900 shp, but these aircraft are being brought to AH.7 standard, with Gems uprated to 1120 shp, thermal-imaging sights, and NVG-compatible cockpits. On 11 August 1986 Westland's Lynx demonstrator with modfications that included BERP III rotor blades set a new world absolute speed record for helicopters of

A Westland Lynx HAS.2 (XZ246/304) about to touch down at RNAS Yeovilton in 1982. Note the toed-out mainwheels, to improve stability on a wet, mobile deck. (Roy Braybrook)

216.45 knots (400.87 km/hr). These new blades and a wheeled undercarriage (in place of skids) are two of main features of the 160 knot (295 km/hr) Battlefield Lynx AH.9, of which 16 are on order to form two squadrons of the new 24 Air Mobile Brigade, which will also have a squadron of eight TOW-Lynx AH.7s and an observation squadron of Gazelles.

The latest version of the land-based Lynx is the Battlefield Lynx AH-9, which has advanced

The Navy Lynx, which proved its value in the Falklands conflict, has been widely accepted, especially by NATO navies. The latest development is the **Super Lynx**, with uprated engines, BERP blades, and 360-degree radar, plus the choice of Sea Skua or Penguin missiles for the anti-ship role. The first order for the Super Lynx came from the Republic of Korea Navy. An anti-ship strike

rotor blades, and a wheeled landing gear in place of skids. (Westland Helicopters).

capability is also offered by the Westland Sea King series: The Indian Navy version can employ Sea Eagle, and both the Pakistan and Egyptian navy versions are equipped for Exocet, as are some of Qatar's Commandos.

For the attack mission the French Army uses the SA.342M Gazelle with Euromissile HOT ATGWs, or a single 20 mm GIAT cannon. Similarly armed Gazelles have been exported to several countries. The French Navy currently does not use helicopters for anti-ship strike, though Exocet arms the Super Frelons of Pakistan and the Super Pumas of Abu Dhabi, Kuwait, Qatar and Singapore. The Lightweight AS.15TT missile arms the Dauphin IIs of the Royal Saudi Navy. Aerospatiale export efforts currently appear to centre on the Panther, which is HOT-capable, but continues the multi-role theme.

Germany's first generation anti-tank helicopter (PAH-1) is the **Bo 105P**, which is armed with HOT and is due to receive a night vision system in the early 1990s. The Spanish Army Bo 105 is also HOT-capable. A proposed German variant of the MBB/Kawasaki BK117 (the A-3M version) is being marketed with provisions for eight HOT missiles and a 12.7 mm Browning in a Lucas chin turret.

France and Germany are jointly developing a second-generation day/night all-weather attack helicopter, a programme that is to be managed by Eurocopter, a company owned by MBB and Aérospatiale. Powered by two 1300 shp MTU/Turboméca/R-R MTM390 engines, this new design is to be built in two versions: the HAP support/escort aircraft for the French Army, and the HAC/PAH-2 anti-tank aircraft for both armies. First flight is scheduled for 1991, leading to deliveries of 75 HAPs beginning in 1997, those of 212 PAH-2s for Germany starting in 1998, and of 140 HACs for France in 1999. The primary role of the **HAP** is to protect the HAC against enemy combat helicopters and slow-flying fixed-wing aircraft, but it will also provide air support for French ground forces.

Left: A Royal Navy Lynx modified to show how the Super Lynx will look, with 360-degree radar and Kongsberg Penguin anti-ship missiles. (Westland Helicopters)

The Aerospatiale SA.342 Gazelle
(F-WTNA, c/n 1185) with six
Euromissile HOT anti-tank
missiles, as shown at
Farnborough in 1976.
(Roy Braybrook)

The Exocet-armed Super Puma,
as exported to at least four
countries. (Aérospatiale)

The second prototype of the
Aérospatiale SA.365M Panther
(F-ZVLO, c/n 6005), at
Farnborough in 1986.
(Roy Braybrook)

The German Army's first
generation anti-tank helicopter
(PAH-1) is the Bo 105P, armed
with HOT missiles. (Euromissile)

The latest mockup of the
Eurocopter PAH-2/HAC/HAP
helicopter, as shown at ILA-88 at
Hanover. The near side
represents the French HAC
version, with four ATGW3
inboard and two Matra AATCP
missiles outboard. (Deutsche
Messe AG, W. Krebs)

The anti-tank HAC/PAH-2 will have eight HOT-2 or TRIGAT air-surface missiles, and four air-air missiles for self-defence (Stingers for Germany, Mistrals for France). It will be equipped with a mast-mounted IR-CCD (charge coupled device) gunner's sight, a nose-mounted IR-CCD pilot's sight, and helmet-mounted sights and displays for both pilot and gunner. In the case of the HAP version, the mast-mounted sight will provide similar thermal-imager, TV and laser-ranger facilities, but will have direct view optics instead of HOT provisions. The pilot will have NVGs, but no thermal imager. The HAP will be armed with a 30 mm cannon in a chin turret, four Mistral air-air GW, and two 22-round RP pods.

Italy is the only European country to have developed an attack helicopter on a national basis. The **Agusta A.129** first flew on 15 September 1983, and an initial batch of 60 is being built for the Italian Army. It is powered by two 944 shp RR.1004 Gem engines, and is armed with a 12.7 mm chin turret and up to eight TOWs. Options include Hellfire and HOT missiles and a mast-mounted sight. The A.129 also forms the basis for the proposed Tonal light attack helicopter, although more powerful engines and more advanced avionics would be used. Tonal is a joint project by Britain, Italy, the Netherlands and Spain. In the context of Italy, it may also be noted that the Italian Navy uses the Sistel Marte anti-ship missile on the SH-3D Sea King, and that the Turkish Navy arms its Agusta-Bell AB.212s with the Sea Skua missile.

The first prototype (E.I.901/MM590) of the A.129 Mangusta (Agusta)

As in the case of most first generation attack helicopters from Western Europe, the Soviet Union has initially favoured multi-role types rather than dedicated anti-tank designs. At the upper end of the range, the Mil Mi-8 Hip, which is powered by two 1700 shp Isotov engines, had been equipped (eg, in Hip-E form) with a 12.7 mm nose gun, six hardpoints for RPs, and four for ATGWs. Seating up to 24 troops in the cabin, the military Mi-8 has no direct equivalent in the West.

The principal Soviet attack helicopter is the **Mi-24 Hind**, which has two 2200 shp engines, the pilot and gunner seated in tandem under separate canopies, and a cabin that can seat up to eight troops, who can fire their guns from the windows. A nose turret mounts a four-barrel 12.7 mm machine gun or a two-barrel 30 mm cannon. The Mi-24 has four underwing hardpoints and provisions for up to eight ATGWs.

The **Mi-28 Havoc** is a dedicated attack helicopter, with no space for troops, although a small compartment in the rear fuselage allows for the recovery of two downed aircrew. The first prototype had its maiden flight on 10 November 1982, but development has been held back by the avionics system, and the example presented at Le Bourget in 1989 is believed to have been a development batch aircraft. The Mi-28 is powered by two Isotov TV3-117 engines, each providing 2,200 shp. Maximum speed is 143 knots (265 km/hr). The Mi-28 is armed with a chin-mounted 30 mm cannon, as used on a BMP-2 vehicle, AT-6 Spiral beam-riding guided weapons, and unguided RPs. Empty weight is approximately 15,435 lb (7,000 kg), and maximum "useful" load (probably meaning warload) is given as 8,025 lb (3,640 kg). Normal take-off weight is 22,930 lb (10,400 kg), and maximum gross is 25,137 lb (11,400 kg).

Photographed in 1983 from a Kaman Seasprite looking for wreckage from the 747 flight KL007 shot down by an Su-25, this Mi-24 Hind E was armed with RP pods and AT-6 Spiral missiles. Note the cloverleaf camouflage. (US Navy)

The Mi-28 Havoc photographed in front of the old control tower at Le Bourget in 1989. (Roy Braybrook)

Kamov helicopters with contra-rotating rotors dominate Soviet naval applications such as ASW and SAR, the two principal types being the Ka-25 Hormone with two 900 shp engines and the Ka-27 Helix (the civil version of which is the Ka-32) with two of 2225 shp.

In an East European context, it may be noted that Romania has developed a lightweight gunship helicopter, the **IAR-317 Airfox**, derived from the Alouette III. It has a single 858 shp Artouste engine, first flew in April 1984, and made its public début at Le Bourget in June 1985.

Returning to the subject of US attack helicopter development, the Bell AH-1 series, which was introduced only as an interim type, has in fact continued in production to the present day. Orders now exceed 1400 units. In US Army service the AH-1G was superseded by the TOW-capable AH-1Q, but this was only an interim standard, pending the AH-1S. Although the USMC had some AH-1Gs, that service demanded a twin-engined TOW-capable version, which led to the AH-1J Sea Cobra with Navy electronics, rotor brake and 20 mm chin turret. The AH-1J was used operationally in SE Asia from February 1971. It was superseded by the AH-1T version, and later by the AH-1W SuperCobra with two T700 engines giving a combined output of 3200 shp. The armament of the AH-1W includes an M197 20 mm cannon and up to eight TOW or Hellfire ATGWs.

In late 1988 the US Army introduced new designations for its AH-1S Cobra/Tow. The AH-1S designation is now retained only for upgraded AH-1Gs. The first 100 new-build AH-1Ss become AH-1Ps, the next 98 AH-1Es, and the final batch, hitherto known as Modernised AH-1Ss, are now AH-1Fs.

Further Bell developments include the Model 406CS (Combat Scout), which is being produced for Saudia Arabia and is derived from the US Army OH-58D, though much of the latter's expensive equipment is deleted. The Army has a small number of armed variants of the OH-58D, some of which were used in night

In civil form the Ka-27 Helix becomes the Ka-32, as represented by this aircraft (CCCP-31000) at Le Bourget in 1985. (Roy Braybrook)

Romania's IAR-317 Airfox is a tandem-seat gunship derivative of the Alouette III. (Roy Braybrook)

A Bell AH-1S, awaiting flight trials on the ramp at Hurst near Fort Worth in 1980. (Roy Braybrook)

operations against Iranian fast patrol boats in the Gulf in early 1988. The mast-mounted sight with TV, thermal imager annd laser designator/ranger is retained, and provisions are made for two 12.7 mm guns, two 7-round RP pods, and up to four Hellfire ATGWs.

In broadly the same size category, McDonnell Douglas exports the 500/530MG Defender in two basic armament variants: the Scout Defender, which may be equipped with a 7.62 mm machine gun, and the TOW Defender with four ATGW pods and an appropriate sighting device. The Nightfox version has a thermal imager and NVG provisions.

However, the principal McDonnell Douglas helicopter is the **AH-64A Apache**, which was selected to fulfil US Army demands for an AAH (Advanced Attack Helicopter). Unquestionably the world's leading day/night all-weather rotary-wing attack aircraft, the AH-64 first flew on 30 September 1975, and deliveries began in early 1984.

The AH-64A is powered by two 1700 shp General Electric T700 engines, and has a maximum level speed of 160 knots (296 km/hr). It has a fixed armament in the form of a ventral-mounted 30 mm M230 Chain Gun for area fire suppression, and can carry up to 16 Hellfire laser-homing ATGWs or 76 FFARs. A nose turret houses the Martin Marietta TADS/PNVS (target acquisition and designation sight, and pilot's night vision system).

Initial operational capability (IOC) was reached in July 1986 by the 3rd Sqn of the 6th Cavalry Brigade, the first of 34 US Army AH-64A combat battalions. In November 1987 AH-64s were delivered to the first National Guard unit: the 1st Battalion, 130th Aviation, North Carolina Army National Guard. In January 1988 the first European based AH-64A battalion was formally activated at Illesheim in West Germany. The US Army plans to deploy 14 AH-64 battalions in Europe by 1992, and to purchase 975 of these helicopters by 1995. Planned developments for the AH-64 include a sensor update, improved air combat capability, a mast-mounted mm-wave radar, and an active mm-wave radar-homing development of Hellfire.

An Israeli Air Force Model 500MG/TOW Defender (serial 206) with nose-mounted sight and bifurcated exhausts. (McDonnell Douglas Helicopter Co)

A heavily-armed AH-64A Apache (serial 22248) at Middle Wallop in 1982. (Roy Braybrook)

In the late 1990s the AH-64 will be augmented by the US Army's **LHX** light scout/attack helicopter, of which it is planned that 2096 will be purchased to replace aircraft such as the AH-1, OH-6 and OH-58. Deliveries are scheduled to begin in 1996.

At time of writing two teams of manufacturers are still competing for LHX: McDonnell Douglas and Bell, rivalling Boeing and Sikorsky. Engine selection has taken place, the contract for the 1330 shp T800 (of which LHX will have two) going to LHTEC (LHX Turbine Engine Co), combining Garrett with Allison. The LHX is to achieve a maximum cruise speed of 170 knots (315 km/hr) and to have provisions for an internal armament of four Hellfire ATGWs and two Stinger air-air missiles. It will also have a turreted gun.

The LHX is to have some 'stealth' features, and will be the US Army's first all-composite metric aircraft. It is to be operable in an NBC environment, and will have digital fibre-optic FBW controls. A mission equipment package (MEP) will be retrofittable to existing Army helicopters, and will include a wide-view helmet-mounted display for the pilot, a digital map and GPS, second generation

The unarmed Bell OH-58D (serial 24693) forms the basis for the US Army's 'AH-58D Warrior' employed in night operations in the Persian Gulf. (Roy Braybrook)

This AH-64A is carrying 16 Hellfires and four Stinger AAMs. On the ground are four fuel tanks, four RP pods and 76 FFARs, twin Stinger installations, one Sidewinder (far left) and one Sidearm (far right). (McDonnell Douglas)

FLIR/EO targeting, and a system to assist in target recognition. In the light attack role it will carry eight Hellfires and two Stingers, in armed reconnaissance four of each, and in the air-air combat role eight Stingers and two Hellfires.

The US Navy has been slow to assign an anti-ship role to its helicopters, but the Kongsberg Penguin Mk 3 sea-skimming missile has now been chosen to arm the Sikorsky S-60B Seahawk. For the longer term, the Navy is studying the possible procurement of 300 Bell-Boeing SV-22A Osprey tilt-rotor aircraft for the ASW role, evidently to replace carrier-based fixed-wing aircraft currently performing such duties. This would be in addition to the 50 V-22As now planned (out of the 913 for the four US services) for naval combat SAR. Since the Lockheed S-3B Viking ASW aircraft has provisions for the anti-ship Harpoon missile, it seems likely that the Osprey will eventually have a similar attack capability.

To summarise, the land-based rotary-wing attack aircraft came of age in Vietnam, and its ship-based equivalent proved its value in the Falklands and the Gulf War. Advances in avionics in the post-Vietnam period have made possible attack helicopters with day/night all-weather performance, and progress in missile technology (eg, in mm-wave radar homing) will bring the fire-and-forget engagement of tanks with minimal dependence on friendly ground forces. Although its development has lagged for many years behind that of its fixed-wing equivalent, the rotary-wing attack aircraft has finally emerged as a formidable weapon system, both over the battlefield and at sea.

This 1/12th-scale model of the Boeing/Sikorsky LHX design illustrated such features as the ventral turret, the retractable GW pallet, and the ducted-fan tail rotor. (Boeing)

Abbreviations

AAA	anti-aircraft artillery
AAC	Army Air Corps (British Army)
AAH	Advanced Attack Helicopter (now AH-64)
AB	air base
ACLS	Automatic Carrier Landing System (Sperry)
ACM	air combat manoeuvres
ADF	automatic direction-finding (aka radio compass)
ADV	Air Defence Variant (Tornado)
AFB	air force base
AFRES	Air Force REServe (USAF)
AFVG	Anglo-French Variable-Geometry (aircraft)
aka	also known as
AM	amplitude modulation
AMRAAM	Advanced Medium-Range Air-Air Missile (now AIM-120)
ANG	Air National Guard (US)
AOA	angle of attack
API	armour-piercing incendiary (ammunition)
ARA	aerial rocket artillery (US Army)
ARBS	Angle Rate Bombing System (Hughes Aircraft)
ARVN	Army of the Republic of VietNam
ASMP	*Air-Sol Moyenne Portée* (Aérospatiale)
AST	Air Staff Target
ASW	anti-submarine warfare
ATA	Advanced Tactical Aircraft (USN)
ATGW	anti-tank guided weapon
BAC	British Aircraft Corp
BAe	British Aerospace
BAI	battlefield air interdiction
BAM	*Base Aérea Militar* (Argentina)
BAP	*Bombe Accéléréе de Pénétration* (Thomson-Brandt)
BERP	British Experimental Rotor Programme
BOBS	Beacon Only Bombing System
BS	Bristol-Siddeley

C/A	coarse acquisition (code)
CAINS	Carrier Airborne Inertial Navigation System (Litton)
CAP	combat air patrol
CAS	close air support
CBU	cluster bomb unit
CCD	charge-coupled device
COIN	counter-insurgency
CONFICS	CObra Night FIre Control System
DH	de Havilland
DMZ	Demilitarized Zone (Vietnam)
ECM	electronic countermeasures
ECR	Electronic Combat and Reconnaissance (Tornado)
FAA	Fleet Air Arm (RN)
FAA	*Fuerza Aérea Argentina*
FAC	forward air control(ler)
FAE	fuel-air explosive
FAMA	*Fábrica Argentina de Materiales Aerospaciales*
FBW	fly-by-wire
FFAR	Folding Fin Aircraft Rocket
FGA	fighter/ground attack
FLIR	forward-looking infra-red
FM	frequency modulation
FMA	*Fábrica Militar de Aviones* (Argentina)
FOL	forward operating location
FSED	full-scale engineering development
GD	General Dynamics
GEC	General Electric Company
GPMG	general purpose machine gun
GPS	Global Positioning System
HAC	*Hélicoptère Anti-Char*
HAP	*Hélicoptère d'Appui-Protection*
HARM	High-speed Anti-Radar Missile (Texas Instruments)
HAS	hardened aircraft shelter
HE	high explosive
HF	high frequency
HUD	head-up display
HVAR	High Velocity Aircraft Rocket
IDS	InterDiction/Strike (Tornado)
ILS	instrument landing system
INS	inertial navigation system

IOC	initial operational capability
IP	initial point
IR	infra-red
Jabo	*Jagdbomber*
LANA	Low Altitude Night Attack
Lantirn	Low Altitude Navigation and Targeting Infra-Red for Night (Martin Marietta)
LBG	laser-guided bomb
LHTEC	LHX Turbine Engine Co. (Garrett and Allison)
LLTV	low-light television
LZ	landing-zone
MAP	Military Assistance Program (US)
MASH	Mobile Army Surgical Hospital (US Army)
MCAS	Marine Corps Air Station (USMC)
MDC	McDonnell Douglas Corp
MEP	mission equipment package
mm	millimetre
MTBF	mean time between failures
MTI	moving target indication
Navstar	navigation system time and range
NBC	nuclear, bacteriological and chemical
NOS	night observation surveillance
NSG	*Nachtschlachtgruppe*
NVA	North Vietnam Army
NVG	night vision goggles
P	precision (code)
PNVS	Pilot's Night Vision System (Martin Marietta)
R&D	research and development
RFC	Royal Flying Corps
RNAS	Royal Naval Air Service
RP	rocket projectile
R-R	Rolls-Royce
RWR	radar warning receiver
SAC	Strategic Air Command (USAF)
SAM	surface-air missile
SAR	search and rescue
SCAS	stability and control augmentation system
SKG	*Schnellkampfgeschwader*
SOS	Special Operations Squadron (USAF)
SOW	Special Operations Wing (USAF)

SS	*sol-sol*
SSB	single-sideband
StG	*Stukagruppe*
STO	short take-off
Stuka	*Sturzkampfflugzeug*
TA	terrain-following
TAC	Tactical Air Command (USAF)
TADS	Target Acquisition and Designation Sight (Martin Marietta)
TBO	time between overhauls
TDY	temporary duty (US services)
TER	triple ejection rack
TF	terrain-following
TF	trench fighter (WWI)
TK	temporary kit
TFS	Tactical Fighter Squadron (USAF)
TFW	Tactical Fighter Wing
TOW	Tube-launched, Optically-tracked, Wire-guided (Hughes Aircraft)
TRAM	Target Recognition and Attack, Multisensor
TRIGAT	Third Generation Anti-Tank (missile by EMDG)
TRN	terrain reference navigation
UHF	ultra-high frequency
USAAC	United States Army Air Corps
USAAF	United States Army Air Force
VBW	Vertical Ballistic Weapon (MBB)
VHF	very high frequency
VNAF	(South) VietNam Air Force
VOR	VHF Omni-directional Range (navaid)
V/STOL	vertical/short take-off and landing
WP	white phosphorus
WW	World War

Index